Luke Hutchinson

Copyright © 2021 Luke Hutchinson

All rights reserved.

ISBN: 9798711435044

Adventurous Living

To Noa,

Contents

	Introduction	9
	Part One	
1	Living In Bubblewrap	21
2	Taking Risks	33
3	Rooted In Confidence	47
4	Leap Of Faith	63
5	Facing Your Family	75
6	Dancing With Resistance	91
	Part Two	
7	Fighting Your Goliath	107
8	Say Yes To Opportunities	121
9	Say No To Tango	133
10	The Beauty Within	145
11	Being Secretly Incredible	161
12	Doing Life Together	173
	Top Tips	183
13	Epilogue	187

Introduction

Carl Allen in *Yes Man* (played by Jim Carrey) is a character that seemed to hate life. He receives an average wage and holds a loathsome job at a loan company that he doesn't like. Carl has shallow friendships who he doesn't enjoy spending time with. He dreads getting up in the morning as he hasn't anything to look forward to. Out of fear he refuses offers that come his way as they would disrupt his routine. His schedule is bleak, his enjoyment is sparse and adventure doesn't exist in his vocabulary.

A friend invites him to a conference where a charismatic preacher singles him out from the audience and coerces him to say yes to everything. From now on Carl wasn't allowed to say no. As the story goes on, this wasn't easy for Carl as he has to do things he doesn't enjoy. But he found that the more he said yes, the more interesting his life got. However, Carl felt that the more giving and sacrificial he was, the more life didn't work out for him. After giving a homeless man a lift, he ran out of fuel for his car. Like any Hollywood love story, a lovely lady passed by and offers him a lift. Carl fell for her and began to see the reward of saying yes, pay off. As love blossomed, so did Carl's ability to agree to opportunities that came his way. However, new to this world of positive thinking, he didn't know how to discern the right time to say yes. Carl said yes to anything and everything and it began to ruin his life. It began to ruin his relationships and his work load became too much.

To cut a long story short, Carl realised saying yes opened up opportunities he could never have imagine (though it was also important for Carl to know when to say no.) His life was seemingly boring and uneventful, but with this new mindset and a promise to himself to say yes, his life changed.

Aside from the dramatised narrative, you may be able to empathise with Carl's life. Many of us have been there with dead-end jobs and the monotonous humdrum of everyday life. Maybe you still are. What *Yes Man* attempts to illustrate and what I wish to recommend is there is an alternative to your ordinary life. It's living adventurously. This is inviting the extraordinary into the ordinary. It is adding a little bit of colour to your life, zest into your decision, excitement into your friendship, vividness to your work and a bit of oomph to your interests. It's not uncommon that we allow things to stop us experiencing life because we're fearful of the unknown and untold as we prefer the safety and security of our environment. We've forgotten what adventure looks and feels like.

Talking about overcoming the barriers to live adventurously requires a definition of what adventure means. The dictionary tells us it's "an unusual, exciting and daring experience" that often relates to a "reckless or hazardous action or enterprise". However, I would like to suggest that living adventurously isn't a one-off occasion when you go on holiday or sign up for a short-term mission trip. Rather it's a lifestyle choice that seeks to experience the fullness of everyday life, as opposed to settling for what you already know.

Adventurous living is woven into the fabric within each of us that is just waiting to be rediscovered. My hope with this book is that it will awaken your hidden but potentially dormant adventurous spirit. I hope it will empower you to experience life by removing the excuses you create. I've met many people who complain about their situation, their work place, their city, their friends, finances or lack of fun - but they don't do anything about it. Either they can't see the bigger picture of life or they're so entrenched in their circumstances that they've given up. At times it can feel like we're wading through a muddy bog, each step takes effort and is immensely frustrating. Understandably, it feels like it's not worth trying at all.

Many of us try to keep up with the rat race because it's all we've known. Our education system has taught us to stick to the straight and narrow, learn the usual things. To study at university, find a regular job and slowly climb our way out of debt. We're bound by fear and seek a safer lifestyle. We don't know what it means to push ourselves to a new challenge or dream achievable goals. We don't consider taking a few risks or leaving our friends and family at home whilst we pursue with new experiences. We live in a neat little box where everything is predictable and protected. I'll be honest; I'm really bored of the thought of a predictable and protected life and it really saddens me when I see friends stuck in this mindset. Of course there's time for safety and security, but I encourage you to push the circumference of your box to be a little bit bigger.

Living adventurously is threefold. Firstly, it's stopping the things that make you unhappy and pursuing the things that give you a greater sense of purpose. This requires intentional introspection and self-analysis. It's likely you already know what makes you happy, but it's likely that there are also things that you'd love, you just haven't discovered yet. To live differently requires you to take risks, which inevitably means leaving your comfort zone.

Secondly, living adventurously is seeking a deeper purpose and meaning to life. This is discovering the rhythm and reason for life which unavoidably leads you to the first point; being happy. Adventure breeds from having a hope and faith in something or someone. Without a context to your adventure, it can feel in vain. Adventurous living is not self-gratification but seeking something bigger than ourselves.

Thirdly, living adventurously is a process in overcoming the barriers we have created. The reason they are barriers is because they prevent us from moving forwards. These barriers are experiences we've had, lies we've believed and misunderstandings we have about life.

> Saying yes underpins adventurous living because it agrees with the wildness of life.

My aim is to open the conversation to help us identify these barriers. The list is not exhaustive, rather personal experiences and general observations. I have not provided a 'how to guide' because the intention is to encourage you to redefine what living adventurously means personally. It's trial and error. Adventurous living is subjective because what might be an adventure to me could be the worst idea of fun for you. Therefore, each topic is approached so you that you can apply it to your own life and circumstances. I encourage you not to compare your idea of adventure with the stories that follow, but allow them to inspire you to decide what a life with purpose means for you.

My hope is that each chapter will be a seed planted as you read the stories and experiences. That seed, I hope and pray, will be watered by your drive and desire to experience more. Some seeds will flourish more quickly and the fruit will be more evident, whereas other seeds will take years to nurture and grow. Both processes are equally good and equally necessary. Life is not a sprint, but a marathon.

The best way to describe these thoughts is a self-applicable narrative. I believe stories and testimonies are powerful ways of communicating. I thoroughly enjoy reading biographies from 19th century missionaries to 21st century athletes. Their lives speak of trial and triumph. My hope in retelling the stories of giants that have paved the way and live amongst us today will compel you to continue to write your own story. Intertwined with these stories I have shared parts of my own journey. I believe we all have something to share and I hope, by sharing my navigation through life, it will inspire you to share yours. We all need to learn from one another.

Saying yes to adventure will change your life. More than just positive thinking, it gives you a reason to wake up each morning, purpose to building friendships, hope in your workplace and spontaneity to your lifestyle. Saying yes underpins adventurous living because it agrees with the wildness of life.

I used to watch *Whose Line Is It Anyway?* when I arrived home from school because I was mesmerised with how the comedians spontaneously created funny scenarios and were able to uphold a hilarious sketch with no script or guidance. A few years later I learnt that there are rules to spontaneous comedy. When one person suggests something mid-flow, for example, you've fallen off your chair and they say, "we'll have to get a bandage for your broken arm", you can't reply, "no, my arm is fine, actually." Why? Because it's not funny. Your response has gone against what the other person spontaneously decided would be the situation and now you've lost the momentum. The rule in spontaneous comedy is to agree with the other person and continue with what they're doing; to go with the flow, so to speak.

You can apply this rule to life. Adventurous living is saying yes and agreeing to whatever comes your way. This then picks up momentum where you can no longer predict the possibilities of life. Saying a simple yes could change the outcome for the rest of your day and potentially your life.

In part one I've identified six barriers which can prevent us from living with purpose. There are many challenges we face, but for me, these have been particularly difficult. Part two gives hope to six ways to live more adventurously. Again, not an exhaustive list, but lessons I've learnt (and am still learning) that I wish to share with you.

Finally, something I remind myself is that I am in control of my own circumstances. There are very few things in my life I couldn't change. My aim is to remind you that you can make decisions for your life and this is the process of redefining purpose for yourself. However, even whilst you're in the driving seat, it's okay to not know what you're doing or where you're going. The importance is that you're wanting to try.

Adventurous living is realising the false expectations and allowing yourself to do things differently. It's introspectively acknowledging the lies you are believing. It's only when you have a perspective, more of a birds eye view on your situation, can you begin to make decisions differently and begin to say yes.

Part One

One

Living In Bubblewrap

Comfort is secretly addictive. Comfort is that feeling when you've been away for a long trip, no doubt exhausted and you see your house for the first time in weeks and can't wait to jump into your comfortable bed. The familiar smells of your house, the favourite spot on the sofa, the availability of food in the fridge, entertainment on demand.

The feeling of comfort is at times important, healthy and necessary but sometimes our lives can become too comfortable. Your comfort zone this is usually the last place adventure occurs. How then, with lives of convenience, do we shake ourselves up and create an appetite to leave our comfort zone and live an adventurous life? The journey of leaving my comfort zone began when I was 17 and decided to leave home.

I remember being terrified driving to my secondary school, because after one year of studying A Levels, I would receive my exams results. I wasn't worried about the results themselves as I knew I had not done well. Rather, I was fearful of my parent's reaction. I was fearful I had let them down and would disappoint them. I never enjoyed school. I had some good friends but I couldn't connect with the teachers and subjects I was supposed to be learning. Because of this, and my inability to communicate my struggles, I became the class-clown.

There's always one. I was that one.

Being an idiot was my way of getting attention, communicating and escaping from the fact that I couldn't learn like my other class mates. My A Level results spoke for themselves. I wasn't naturally academic and a traditional school didn't suit my style of learning. Unfortunately the UK mainstream education system, although it tries, simply doesn't accommodate those with a bit more energy. I didn't have a short attention span, I just didn't care about what I was learning. As a teenager, I couldn't foresee how finding 'X' would help me climb trees or play football better. How can learning about meandering rivers help me pay bills in the future?

Quite simply, I wasn't cut out for school and studying A Levels was too hard for me. My mother (the wise woman that she is) knew this as well and began searching for other things I could do. At 17, your horizons are pretty narrow. You don't consider the implications of quitting school and trying something new. At that age, doing anything from the normal trend seemed like the equivalent of turning up to PE without your sports kit. – it isn't recommended. Little did I know how breaking the norm would open up opportunities I couldn't have dreamed of.

At the age of 17 I decided to move from Doncaster to Plymouth; opposite ends of the country and very different places to live. I told my mother I would be interested in moving out like my older siblings. Being open to change was the first step.

Whilst in my last year of school I downloaded music software on my father's hand-me-down Windows XP computer. I soon learnt that I could upload a track and mix it with another one with added reverb or delay. There was a sync button that matched the tracks together and with a slow pull of the fader it made seamless transition into another track. After playing back, often surprised at what I would hear, I figured I was a professional music DJ. My career was set. I figured my tracks needed vocals so bought myself a USB microphone to plug into the computer. Music. That was going to be my thing. After explaining my new passion to my mum, doing what she does best, she took me at my word and began researching for music colleges. There were a few nearby but she decided we should visit one in Plymouth starting in two months and six hours away in the car. I knew, being the youngest of four siblings, I would have to leave home at some point but I didn't think it would be as soon as this.

We visited the college in Plymouth, the city that sent many teams of adventurers into undiscovered areas in the world, and the city where my parents first met while my father served in the Navy. It turned out that the college was just around the corner from where my father proposed to my mum! Life has those strange crossover points.

Upon arriving at the college, I was overwhelmed with the number of mixing desks and sound equipment. Studio after studio full of state of the art paraphernalia and expensive technology. This was the coolest place ever. I knew I wanted to go to this college. For some reason, the prospect of leaving home, leaving friends and the familiarity of Doncaster didn't even cross my mind. When you know what you want, the details start to become a little less important.

My father, an inspiring man and loving husband, sometimes reminds me of that season when I decided I'd leave home. He reminds me that I used to talk about life as if I'd stay at home for as long as I could. I vaguely remember this as well. I liked my home after all. I had no reason to leave. I liked the idea of eventually leaving school, buying a car, finding a job and being able to return home having a meal waiting on the table for me. What 17-year-old would complain about that lifestyle? I have fond memories of playing football in the back garden and building go-karts with my brother in the garage. We were fortunate to have our back garden next to an unused quarry where we'd take our bikes and race down the hills. In the winter if it snowed well, we would take our sledges and anything else we figured would allow us to slide and dare one another to go down the steepest hill. As my brother and I grew older we took up golf and set ourselves at the top of the hill and played until we lost all our golf balls from driving them into the open fields. That was a quarry of adventure that I hope my kids will have something similar to.

So why would I suddenly want to leave all this? Why did all those memories and fun times seem like distant memory with the prospect of a new adventure? At the time I didn't know what my motivation was. But now looking back I realise I was driven by the desire to explore and experience more. After visiting Plymouth it made me realise that change is possible and I no longer needed to live within the confines I had put on myself. I began to dream of the possibilities.

Two months later before the term began, with £250 in my back pocket and all of my belongings in the back of the car, my parents drove me to Plymouth for the second time as I embarked on an adventure that would change my life. I had no experience of living on my own or even sharing accommodation (with eight other people). I had no wisdom in how to navigate and learn the culture of a new city and of course I lacked a little bit of judgement. But it was this innocent naivety that removed the fears and worries. I wasn't asking questions, I was just driven by the taste of independence and motivated by the feeling of finding my purpose. When my parents asked if I wanted to go, I just said yes.

On reflection, maybe that's an attitude we need to adopt more often. Not caring, or even being naïve. It has bad connotations attached to it, but I often wonder where our lives will go if we chose to be more naïve and have less attachment to being comfortable. To ask less questions and just do. I wonder if it will make our lives more fun if choose not to worry or over complicate things?

Actually, I know it will make life more fun.

I watched a TV an episode from *Escape to the Wild* presented by Kevin McCloud when he visited a British family living in Chile... next to a volcano. This wasn't six hours away, but over six thousand kilometres away. The parents, Jago who worked in IT, and Lucy, a city lawyer, used to live in London with their three children. They experienced the humdrum of city life like thousands of people do each day. Jago describes the London lifestyle as, "keeping up with the rat race" and couldn't see themselves doing the same thing in twenty years' time, so they decided to break from the routine.

The family sold their home in London, bought a converted rally support truck and hit the road living off their savings. Their motivation was to spend more time with their children before they grew up as they would naturally become less interested in their parents. Lucy observed as parents they felt "less stressed and less busy... so the children could be happier." Their new lifestyle required them to be self-sustainable and quite literally 'living off the land'. They had begun to build their house embedded into a hill and collected rock, wood and mud mixed with straw to construct their new home. Each piece of wood that made up the house had been hand-selected by Jago with the help of native locals. The views overlooked mountains as far as the eye could see accompanied with the volcano protruding itself not so far away. Their life was simple. No technology, simple machinery, small community and beautiful surroundings. It was tranquil, except for the occasional earthquake and threat of the volcanic eruptions.

But still, what makes a family relocate from England to South America to one of the most hostile and physically demanding environments on the planet and build a mud house to live in? Surely that cannot be comfortable? Jago reflected on his life in London, "You're immediately wrapped up in the pressures of life, you don't get that here. It's a much easier and friendly way of life."

For me, I crave a slower pace of life that is less complicated. A life more in touch with nature; dependent on the raw materials around us and less dependent on the unnecessary consumer products we are bombarded with. A life with less pressure. My guess would be that you desire a life with

> Being open to change
>
> was the first step.

meaning and purpose - not one with aimless goals and unfulfillment.

It was interesting to see Kevin McCloud baffled when he met the family and dumbstruck as to why they had moved so far away, with such a high risk of living in the shadow of a volcano. In the closing scenes of a panoramic view as the sun sets over the volcano, the parents share a glass of wine and the children joyfully play with one another, Kevin McCloud reflects, "I thought you were mad for living here. I don't think there are many people like you. There are not many people who will venture that far. They can do stuff here that makes them feel really alive. I really admire people like that because they take their family and show them what is possible, what is out there, an alternative. I could see that people may look at Jago and Lucy and think how mad they are at giving up successful careers and a stable urban life … they've smashed through that comfort zone. That seems to be the key to their happiness, actually."

Perhaps that's why it can be difficult to live adventurously - because we've created comfort around us. What if we pushed ourselves a little more?

To do things we care more about even if it means sacrificing some of our comforts. Consider what it would take for you to lay aside some of your comforts to begin that project or apply for that job you've always wanted. The first step is to acknowledge your preference for comfort is holding you back from building deeper friendships, pursuing an interest or hobby or giving your time volunteering. Don't feel bad, just do something about it.

If it helps, begin to get practical about your comfort (and in chapter four, your fears). In one column make a list of things you would like to do or achieve in the next few months or the next years. In the second column write down what is holding you back from make progress towards them. You can take this one step further and begin identifying what lies you are believing about yourself.

More than often we choose comfort because it's easier. Comfort at times is needed. But if you're wanting to live more adventurously you may find it hard to do so if your life is wrapped in bubblewrap.

Two

Taking Risks

Every day we are faced with decisions to make. Usually quite small ones like what cereal to have for breakfast or which coffee shop to get our caffeine fix. Throughout life we often face larger choices and decisions about jobs, careers, relationships and where to live. For some the power of decision making is taken away – but for many of us, our future is in our hands and is entirely up to us. Often making a decision is taking a risk.

If you are anything like me, you'll steer well clear of danger. But what if danger presents itself to you and there's no way of escaping? Will you fight or flight? Taking a risk is difficult because you don't know the outcome. But how adventurous would our lives look if we never stepped out because we were fearful of the result? Perhaps not very.

During a summer's day with a few friends, I was involved in a situation that took a turn for the worst and I was presented with a few risky decisions I needed to make. They weren't big life decisions, but they were decisions that involved a lot of risk.

Living in Plymouth in the summer is one of best places to be. It has the best of three worlds: city, beach and country. On a scorching day with my friends Mairi and Seb, we decided to visit the beach. Bantham, like many beaches along the Devon coast line, is hidden from the public eye and requires a drive through iconic country lanes that make you wince every time a car narrowly passes by. Bantham is a well-known spot for longboard surfers as the waves tends to be fairly small, though on this occasion we didn't surf but went for a walk – little did we know what was in store for us.

Summer is my favourite season of the year. I can sense the mood of people lift ever so slightly. The summer makes me happy. Summer also breeds adventure – the sort of adventure where you jump in a car and let the rest of the day work itself out. It was mid-afternoon when we arrived at Bantham beach (fortunately without Mairi damaging her the paintwork on her car) and we piled out, grabbing our bags and Seb bringing our skateboards. Why we took our skateboards to the beach, I've no idea. We walked down the paths towards to the sand and agreed to head towards Burgh Island off the headland of Bantham.

We walked along the half-mile sandy beach that stretches towards the Island; a piece of land that stands out from the coastland as if it is trying to separate itself from the rest of England. As soon as our feet touched the warm sand, it was if all the worries and concerns of life evaporated. I love that feeling. You can't be stressed whilst at a beach. With our sights set on Burgh Island, we made our way across a small estuary which, at the time, seemed more like a tiny stream coming from the sea moving inland. It was only ankle deep and it's common to cross the stream that then connects with the rest of beach which leads to the island.

Without a second thought, we began our ascent up the hill of the island with anticipation as to what the views at the top could offer us. It was quite an easy walk with marked out tracks and paths to follow. Burgh Island at some point must have been a military look out point as the top is scattered with remnants of old buildings and bunkers. If you walk on a little further toward the edge of the island, you find yourself separated from the noise of children and camera clickers. This was the spot we were looking for. Before sitting down, we turned around to soak in the views of the beaches on both sides of the island and observed the small humans that looked like ants going about their business. With soft grass beneath our feet we sat down and looked out to sea, staring at the blue paints strokes of sky and breathed in the fresh ocean air. There's nothing quite like it.

There's no adventure like sitting on the edge of an island with no one around except your close friends. Seb, suggested descending the other side of the island to find out what was there. I hesitated. Anyone with common sense would see that the marked-out path had ended, and the only way down was to climb the rocks. Trusting his idea of fun, I let him lead the way, thinking that if anything happened, I would stop following. The only problem with climbing down rocks is that you can't make a judgement whether you can climb back up. At least I can't. That wasn't a worry now; I was just trying to keep up with Seb that sped on ahead. Before I knew it, we had reached the bottom where the sea met the island. If the coastguards saw us now, I don't think they would be best pleased. I got a sense that not many people had been where Seb and I were standing now. With our backs to the island (which was now a collection of rocks) we looked out to sea once more, dreaming of a job where we'd be paid to explore places no one had yet been. Though it was clear the seagulls had beaten us to our secret spot, as their excrement was everywhere. This didn't worry us, we felt like pioneers.

After waving to a group of paddle boarders who passed us by in the water, I suggested to Seb we should make our way back up – figuring that it would probably take longer than he realised. With all our excitement, we had lost sense of time, and I could see that the sun was lowering and realised Mairi was probably getting a bit lonely sat on the top of the island by herself. Leading the expedition, we safely and reassuringly reached the soft grass once again. On greeting Mairi, we couldn't wait to tell her where we had been. Little did we know it wouldn't be the only story we would tell our friends that day.

With our bellies rumbling and the sun going down, we figured it was best to make our way back along the stretch of beach where the car was parked. Making it down the hill where we had walked up, I could immediately see the tide had come in further than I thought it would. Come to think of it, I didn't know what the tide was doing that day. Usually when surfing with friends, there's a few factors we have to take into account, the ground swell, the direction and strength of wind, the distance the swell has been travelling for and… the tide. We walked across the first part of the beach with the intention to walking across the estuary (the tiny stream) to join Bantham beach. When reaching the stream, we realised it wasn't a stream at all, but it looked more like a river as it had grown considerably. The direction of the fast current was going inland and swimming across where the sea joined the river was out of the question. I couldn't work out how deep the estuary was, but I guessed that it was above head height. Without another other option, we continued to walk along the riverbank that led us to the back of the beach that was covered in small sand dunes. It was a small detour, nothing to worry about I thought. Mairi didn't share the same opinion.

We zigzagged along the river to the point where we knew we had to cross to get to the other side. From our side of the river, still facing out to sea we could see the rear of Bantham beach which had now turned into dunes that housed small cottages – and on the other side, to our left, there was a large wall which led to the back of a pub (this was over 500 meters along the bank). In that moment we did not fully understand our predicament. The situation was worse than we imagined. How on earth were we going to get to the other side? It was around 5-6pm and most people had left the beach already. We walked along the riverbank hoping there was a bridge that would lead us over. There was nothing. The three of us shared our opinions and options. The only two were; to either walk around to the next bridge or swim across the river. At one point Seb suggested the idea of staying on the beach for a night, building a fire, constructing a shelter and hunting for animals with spears fashioned from the raw materials around us. It wasn't a bad idea, but not exactly a realistic one.

On our left, where the pub was located, we noticed a man climbing into a kayak with someone joining him in the back. What a relief! They both paddled in our direction; after all they had probably seen three youngsters stranded on the wrong side like helpless baby turtles trying to find their way home. As the people in the kayak came closer we could see it was an older man rowing at the front with a younger woman in the rear. Father and daughter perhaps? We assumed they would pull up right in front of us and become the answer to all our problems – instead they went straight past. Ceasing the opportunity, we called out asking for help. The man replied the only way across was a bridge, 4 miles down the riverbank (an 8 mile round trip back to the car!) . He dropped his daughter off exactly where we needed to be and rowed back down the river to the pub. We were puzzled. It's as if he knew precisely the problem we had, but couldn't wait till he got back to the pub to tell his friends to watch some idiots decide what to do! Whilst we watched our potential angel pass us by, I realised the estuary had grown even more. Our end goal was becoming even further away.

We had two options. Swim or walk. Fight or flight. Play it safe or take a risk.

To my disbelief, Seb called out, "Hey! Guys! Look what I've found!"

Seb, using his initiative, had searched our immediate area for resources to use. He had found, amidst the dunes, a kayak! We couldn't believe it. I ran over to where Seb was and gave him a hand pulling out a once-loved kayak. The kayak was worse for wear and had every reason to be thrown away. With our options minimal, we could not complain. As if the situation no longer mattered, Seb and I threw the kayak into the water and jumped in with a spirit of optimism. No sooner had our backsides hit the bottom of the kayak, so too had the kayak hit the bottom of the riverbed. We fished it out and allowed the seawater to run out through the holes in the bottom. The kayak could sit on top of the water but could not take much weight.

What would Bear Grylls do? That's what I often think when I'm in situations like this. I suggested to my fellow survivors that walking to a distant bridge was not an option because we didn't know where it was as we'd have to walk along the country roads and by that time it would be dark and dangerous.

The other option I presented to my band of brothers was to put our bags and skateboards into kayak and swim to the other side. I figured that the kayak would act as a large buoyant object that would both hold our valuable possessions and give us something to hold onto. I also recommended taking our t-shirts off (this would be optional for Mairi) so that we had something dry to wear when we reached the other side. I think this is what Bear Grylls would do. We calculated that due to the severity of the current we would be pulled down stream, so we selected a spot on the other side of the bank we wanted to reach and took our position with the kayak 10 meters up stream.

People often say that British sea is cold. Let me tell you this was freezing! Deceivingly it was Summer time, but it was not post-Summer when the sea warms up and now the sun had gone down there was nothing to warm us.

> Do we choose the predictable or do we take a risk?

Without too much hesitation and a short pep talk of 'kick hard!' – we waded our way into the estuary and we pushed off the riverbed when we could walk no further. Leading the team from the front by holding rope attached to the kayak, I developed a technique of a one-arm paddle and crazy leg kicking. Mid-paddle, I glanced over to Mairi who appeared to be hanging onto the kayak for dear life and was contributing very little to the trajectory of the kayak. In the very same moment I remembered Seb couldn't swim. I commend him for not reminding us of his inability to swim as we all mutually decided to *swim* across an estuary – I could only imagine that he was hanging on for dear life too.

So here I was, enjoying my summer break in Plymouth deciding to have a pleasant stroll along the beach. What on earth was I doing in a freezing estuary, clinging to a sinking kayak trying to swim?! This wasn't how the day was supposed to go. Once we hit the middle of the river, the current shot us down the riverbank 40 meters further than we expected – but eventually we reached the other side, shivering but relieved. Ditching the kayak and re-clothing ourselves, we walked the steps to the back garden of a cottage, hopped the fence, ran through the garden and joined the road that led us to the car park. We lived to tell the tale.

Everyday, we are faced with decisions to make. Do we choose the predictable or do we take a risk? Realistically, we calculated that we weren't putting our lives into too much danger, as we knew with the kayak; we would reach the other side eventually. But would I be telling you this story if we had chosen to walk to a potentially mythical bridge? Saying yes to an adventure is stepping into the unknown, calculating the risks, trusting your instincts and going for it. Risk is knowing when to fight and when to flight.

There's an inspiring and moving story of Chris McCandless (documented in a book called *Into the Wild*) about a young American who dropped out a college, burnt all his money, ditched his car and went hiking in Canada. His story is one of controversy and risk as he sought the need for risk and adventure. His attitude could be matched with that of ignorance and foolishness, but his desire for adventure is something we all have buried deep within us. *Into The Wild* documents how Chris McCandless' desire for adventure did not go as well as he hoped. He did reach where he wanted to go, but did not calculate the risk as he ought to. He camped in an abandoned trailer next to a swamp, ate the wrong wild plants which made him seriously ill and had no way of communicating with the outside world. He unfortunately died in the trailer. McCandless made the wrong judgements.

Whilst McCandless made a fatal error, his understanding of adventure and risk were admirable. In a letter to his friend Ron, who he met along his journey, he wrote down some of his philosophy.

"So many people live within unhappy circumstances and yet will not take the initiative to change their situation because they are conditioned to a life of security, conformity and conservatism, all of which may appear to give a peace of mind, but in reality nothing is more damaging to the adventurous spirit within a man than a secure future. The joy of life comes from our encounters with new experiences, and hence there is no greater joy than to have an endlessly changing horizon, for each day to have a new and different sun."

If we are fearful of making the wrong judgements and allow it to paralyse our decision making it's likely we'll forever stay comfortable. I'm not advocating to put your life in danger. However, I have found that adventurous living errs on the side of taking risks. Doing so is pushing ourselves out of our comfort zone which can often mean taking the more difficult or unknown route.

It's commonly quoted that "without risk, there's no reward". Naturally we want to know how things will turn out and for the most part, this is sensible. However, it becomes an issue when we allow being risk-averse to swallow up any sense of fun. If avoiding risk at all costs dominates our decision making, it's possible we will live with regrets.

Begin to consider decisions you've made recently and if you chose the safer option because it outcome was predictable. Was there an alternative to that decision that could have opened up doors for you in the future? Are there any calculated risk you could take now which could allow you to live more adventurously?

Redefining your purpose is all about taking risks. It's very much the cliche of 'breaking the mould'. Friends and family will always have an expectation of you and think they know what's best for you. But perhaps you're beginning to realise that isn't the purpose you want for yourself.

In the words of Carl Medearis, "Adventure is a risky journey with an uncertain future. If we know all the answers, it's no longer a risk and thus not really an adventure."

Three

Rooted In Confidence

Having spent my early teenage years training in swimming and badminton, competing in county galas and tournaments around England, I admire (though barely understand) the resilience, determination, passion required of the world's best athlete's. I'm fascinated by what it takes for athletes to put themselves through gruelling training programmes and to sacrifice so much. This self-belief is compelling because it shows what's possible with the right mindset. I'm not talking about arrogance, but more the deep rooted belief that you can achieve what you set your mind to.

Self-belief is a barrier to adventurous living because it prevents us from believing in ourselves. If we don't believe we can achieve our goals, why would we bother trying? If we don't believe we have the skills and competency, what's the point in giving it a go? Self-belief is trusting that you are good enough. Perhaps there's lessons we can learn from a fighter called Ronda Rousey who competed in a sport called MMA (Mixed Martial Arts).

MMA is a full contact sport that combines the use of both striking and grappling techniques including various styles such as wrestling, judo, kickboxing and Muay Thai. MMA is one of the most physical and mentally demanding sports that is increasing in popularity around the world.

Ronda pioneered the Women's division against all speculation that women would never fight in the UFC (Ultimate Fighting Championship). She has finished 10 of her 12 fights in under a minute. Ronda's success has led to movie roles featuring in The Expendables 3, Furious 7, Entourage and also appearing in WWE. She's the first female UFC Champion, the first Olympic medalist to hold a UFC title, has the fastest finish in UFC history, held the longest winning streak in UFC. In 2014 and 2015 she received the Best Female Athlete ESPY Award. Whilst Ronda's road to success is far from over, her journey has not been an easy one.

When Ronda was born, she nearly died. She was delivered with the umbilical cord wrapped around her neck which contributed to a speech disorder as she grew up. Her parents, living in California at the time, moved to North Dakota when Ronda was three years old so she could receive intense speech therapy. For much of her younger years she struggled to communicate and found other ways of doing this.

In a tragic moment on a winter's day, Ronda father took the family sledging. On an ordinary hill, on an ordinary sledge, her father tested the hill and hit a bump on the way down causing the sledge to stop. He remained still, laying in the snow. Her father developed a rare bleeding disorder called Bernard-Soulier syndrome which makes it difficult for the body to form blood clots. In 1991, he was discharged from hospital but was never the same. His spine began to disintegrate and the chronic pain was getting worse. The situation became too much for Ronda's father and he committed suicide.

Ronda had been on a swimming team for years but stopped after her father died. Swimming was too introspective. The first time she stepped on the judo mat she fell in love immediately. Ronda was amazed at the complexity of judo, how intricate it was and the problem solving it required. Judo was the opposite of swimming - you have to be in the present moment and there is no time for thinking. After learning judo for only a month, Ronda entered her first local tournament and won all her matches by instant wins (ippons). Two weeks later in her second tournament, she came second to a junior national champion. Ronda's mother, equally driven and passionate about competing, told her after her first loss, "You are a skinny blonde girl who lives by the beach, and unless you absolutely force them to, no one is ever going to expect anything from you in this sport. You prove them wrong."

Ronda, in her book *My Fight Your Fight*, reflecting on this time in her life remembers, "I was ashamed that I been so ready to accept losing, to accept as a fact that someone else was simply better than me. The remorse lasted only a second before it was replaced by a more intense emotion. What I felt was a deep desire to win, a motivation to show everyone on the planet that no one should ever doubt my ability to win again. From that moment on, I wanted to win every time I stepped onto the mat. I expected to win. I would never accept losing again."

This went on to set the course for her life. Ronda went to extreme lengths to make sure she was training and dieting for judo in the most effective way. She left home at a young age to live with her coach and forced her body to cope with the demanding requirement to weigh a certain amount. Ronda competed as often as she could in her teenage years, defeating anyone put in her way. She was quickly identified as someone with huge potential. Relationship difficulties with her mother forced her to move away from home and embrace a lifestyle of sofa surfing and training daily. Ronda did whatever it took to train in the best places with the best coaches.

She had her sight set on the 2008 Olympics and believed she could win. Commenting on this stage in her life, Ronda remarks, "People talk about how I'm so arrogant. They don't realise how much work went into getting where I am. I worked so hard to be able to think highly of myself. People want to project their own insecurities on others, but I refuse to allow them to put that on me. Just because you don't think that you could be the best in the world doesn't mean that I shouldn't have the confidence to believe I can do anything."

Ronda went onto the win a bronze medal at the 2008 Olympics and became the first American to win an Olympic medal in women's judo. It was immensely disappointing and frustrating for Ronda to not achieve what she had spent years training for, which sent her into a time of searching for meaning and purpose. She eventually found this purpose after watching a UFC fight and thought, "I could beat any one of those".

Ronda began her amateur career in MMA, holding three jobs and training in between. She describes this season of her life as 'hustling' as she knew she could be where she wanted to, but also knew it would take hard work and time to get there. Her self-belief motivated her to get up earlier in the morning and stay late to train.

Ronda went on to fight in the UFC and showed incredible performances and is continuing to impress fans and inspire women to take up MMA. Ronda's belief in herself is an extreme example of what can happen when we're driven by a goal. She was convinced in her own abilities and capabilities. She wasn't distracted or put off by critics that said she could never achieve what she wanted. If anything, she allowed this to spur her on even more. Today Ronda is esteemed as one of the greatest athletes because of what she been able to achieve in a short space of time.

When I read about her life, I believe her success is rooted in her confidence. This speaks volumes when we consider the implications of this in our own lives. It's common to experience moments where we dream and aspire to achieve more. As soon as the dream enters your mind, the voice of doubt speaks up and whispers, "you're not good enough! You could never do that!" When you think of your dreams, your challenges and goals; as soon as doubt creeps in, you have to force it out just as quickly.

At the beginning of Ronda's biography, she allows a glimpse into her frame of mind,

> "Achieving greatness is a long and arduous battle that I fight every day. Fighting is how I succeed. I don't just mean inside a 750-square-foot cage or within the confines of a 64-square-meter mat. Life is a fight from the minute you take your first breath to the moment you exhale your last. You have to fight the people who say it can never be done. You have to fight the institutions that put up the glass ceilings that must be shattered. You have to fight your body when it tells you it is tired. You have to fight your mind when doubt begins to creep in. You have to fight systems that are put in place to disrupt you and obstacles that are put in place to discourage you. You have to fight because you can't count on anyone else fighting for you. You have

to fight for people who can't fight for themselves. To get anything of real value, you have to fight for it."

I was a church youth worker for five months when I returned to the UK after a year of studying in the Netherlands. At least I thought I was a youth worker as this is what was outlined in my job description, but I was actually working with children. This is a very different role requiring different skills. I struggled for five months working in a job I was not good at. For a period of time, I thought I was in the job because I needed to stretch my skills and increase my ability to work with different ages. Though as time went on, I became less passionate and I resented going into work each day.

As well as being in a role that I didn't want to do, I was working on my own. I had taken over from a volunteer who had been working a few days a week from home and a few days in the church. I was their first full time employee. When I arrived there was no office space, no desk or computer. Initially, I didn't let this discourage me, I saw it as an opportunity to pioneer my own role within the church and within the first week I created my own office in a spare room on the church balcony and convinced the Vicar to buy me a second hand Macbook. In the first month I knew the job was not what I expected and by the second month I knew I couldn't do the job for long.

Although I was welcomed by the church community, there was a sense that I was the 'dogsbody' for the church. It was also my role to clear away all the chairs, sweep the floors and remove everyone's rubbish. I got the impression, now there was a paid member of staff, everyone would just let me clear up after them because I was getting paid to do it. I spent most of my time tidying before I could start my tasks for the day. It's quite a miserable feeling when you walk in the cold church on a miserable winter's day and know you have to shift a bunch of table and chairs. I know there's worst things in life to experience, but this was my current situation, and I didn't enjoy it.

In my five months at the church, I don't remember receiving one word of affirmation from the Vicar, my line manager. It's likely he did praise me for the occasional thing I did well, but the negativity from our working relationship outweighed anything positive. The Vicar was a great person who most people spoke highly of. He had done great things and even received a letter from the Prime Minister congratulating him for the work he was doing in the community. But not many people had to spend all week with him, like I did.

I quickly got the impression that he liked to be controlling which meant that I was never able to run with an idea or project without him limiting what I was able to do. In the fourth month I handed in my resignation without another job lined up because I knew I had to leave as soon as I could. I took a risk and fortunately found another job as a mental health support worker after two weeks.

I had to get out of the situation because it was destroying me. My confidence and self-belief had been shattered. I felt I was being treated like a teenager and my gifts and skills weren't acknowledged in the slightest - more so, I didn't have an opportunity in five months to do what I was good at. I knew I had to leave the job because I was believing things about myself that weren't true. In my journal on the 23rd May 2015, I wrote some of the lies I had been believing about myself because of the situation:

> *I don't have any potential. I'm inexperienced and don't understand. My thoughts and opinions don't matter. I don't have anything to offer. I'm incompetent and unable to do things well on my own. I should not keep trying when I get something wrong.*

The truth is, you are good at something, if not a lot of things, and you should be self-assured in that.

After acknowledging the lies I believed, I continued to journal by forgiving the church and the Vicar for not valuing me, treating me like I was young and not allowing me space and room to work. I forgave him for not affirming what I had done well, not training and developing me and speaking down to me.

When I began to search myself and discover why I was discontent and unhappy, I realised it was because I no longer believed in myself. I knew I needed to rediscover purpose for myself. I've no doubt you've experienced situations where you aren't valued and appreciated like you should be. It can feel like we experience a thick fog of disappointment that impacts our self-esteem and confidence.

If you struggle in believing in yourself and don't feel you're good at being you, it's possible that it's because you've once been told that you're not good enough. And unfortunately chosen to believe that lie. At times, we trust someone else's judgement better than our own.

It's not uncommon that you don't just believe one lie about yourself, but through experiences and situations, there is a build up of lies you have accepted. Picture your life as a game of Jenga where you have to pull out a small wooden block without allowing the tower to fall over. Imagine each time a situation or person causes you to believe a lie about yourself, one of the wooden blocks is removed from the tower. Eventually, as you believe more and more lies, the tower becomes increasingly unstable and incomplete.

When I was walking through Brighton where there is often a weird and wonderful collection of people busking or preforming, on this occasion there was a young lad, no older than twelve years old, preforming with his diabolo. Initially all I saw was an orange diabolo hurling through the air, twenty metres high, I then realised it was a young man busking for change from the passing public. I stopped with my friend Hannah and praised him for using his initiative to earn a bit of cash on his Sunday afternoon. I dropped in some change I had and as we walked away it struck me that this busker is the epitome of what our culture is lacking.

More specifically, what is often lacking in us. He was confident enough in his own ability to perform with his diabolo that he took his skills to the street to share it with the world. He didn't allow fear of failure to be an excuse nor he didn't allow his age to prevent him - he had belief in himself that he had something to offer.

Self-belief in the right portion is empowering whilst a lack of it cripples us. It can easily be confused with arrogance or vanity.

Self-belief is acknowledging the things we're good at and being confident in ourselves.

The truth is, you are good at something, if not a lot of things, and you should be self-assured in that. Every human is uniquely and specifically created, with gifts and skills that the world needs to benefit from. You could be gifted with numbers, skilled at communicating, incredible at sports, fantastic at selling products or a talented leader.

Having self-belief enables us to overcome the barrier to living an adventurous life because it means you trust in your talents. There is no reason why you shouldn't. Our culture has painted over self-belief with brush strokes of pride or egotism. Our society doesn't like it when someone sticks their head out from the crowd or displays their greatness to others.

We've forgotten how to appreciate how amazing people are, possibly because we're jealous or insecure. I'd like to correct that by explaining that believing in yourself is a key to enjoying and getting the most out of life.

The truth is, we all have something to offer. The question is, do we believe in it? When we choose to believe in ourselves we overcome the barrier to live an adventurous life.

Four

Leap Of Faith

I fear drowning, more specifically I fear big waves. When I lived in Plymouth I met some incredible friends who taught me how the skate, to appreciate starry nights, to have evenings of fun without alcohol and to acknowledge the beauty of a creation. They showed me the purpose in caring for the poor and being involved in something bigger than myself.

A few of my friends also taught me how to surf. Surfing is seen as one of those 'cool' sports for hippies. What many people don't realise is that you only surf 1% of the time you're in the water. It's common to wait at least 15 minutes for a good wave and then only ride the wave for 10 seconds.

Surfing is standing on a board whilst carving smoothly through a rolling hill of water that is wonderfully created by nature because of the gravitational pull of the Moon that has travelled thousands of miles. What surfing really consists of is lots of paddling through water and sitting on your board staring at a vast blue ocean. Whilst that doesn't sound all that bad - there is a risk to pay for riding waves. To get to the position so you can catch the full length of the wave you have to paddle through the white water (the foamy stuff). The technique to get 'out back' took me months to learn. The idea is you have to push your board underneath the wave so you allow the power of the wave to go over you, so you don't get pushed backwards. What you experience underneath the water for a brief few moments is both incredible and scary.

When you see a wall of water coming towards you, you must time it correctly by pushing your surfboard under the water. If you time it wrong, the wave will crash onto (and most likely through you) which pushes you down towards the seabed. It feels like you're in a washing machine being thrown around losing all sense of direction. The feeling is terrifying. You usually forget to take a deep breath and now underwater, you wonder when you'll rise to the surface. You kick your legs like mad but don't actually know whether you're kicking yourself further down or towards the top.

The key I've learnt after many times of being held down by the power of waves is to grab your ankle that is attached to the leash (a type of cord) which is connected to the board. Fortunately, the surfboard is more buoyant than our bodies and it will find its way to the surface sooner.

It's frustrating because an activity I enjoy so much, I fear just as much. When I used to get picked up in the early morning so we could arrive at the beach for first light, I would spend the entire time on the toilet suffering from a 'nervous poo', whilst the others strapped the boards to the car. I feared being held down by the waves that much, just the thought of it affected me!

For me it was a real fear. The thought of a large wave appears on the horizon about to crash in front of me with the intent of throwing me around like a rag doll. Drowning is a normal fear, just like the fear of heights, aeroplanes, needles, crowds of people, small spaces and insects. It's okay to acknowledge this type of fear. But how do we manage ourselves when we're dominated by irrational fears? Worries we have about things that aren't true or haven't happened. Anxiety stems from the desire for control and knowing how something will turn out. When we're on the journey of finding our purpose it's important not to be governed by irrational fears.

I used to work with young people on a twelve-week program to boost their confidence and give them necessary skills to find employment afterwards. It was a privilege to see how much progress they made and how their whole character and self-belief grew over the twelve weeks. When I recall the initial interviews; they often appeared shy, anxious and quiet. Often through no fault of their own, they grew up in families and communities that have put boundaries and expectation onto them which has flattened their self-esteem. Many of the young people I worked with weren't given permission to dream or believe they could achieve anything.

More often than not, they were gripped by fear. Many of the young people didn't have a social life or spend much time outdoors. A handful didn't have parents who genuinely cared for them and left them gaming all day. Whilst other parents tried to wrap their teenager in cotton wool.

On the first day of the programme I had a group of teenagers quietly sat around a table playing ice-breakers so we could learn each other's names. Somehow it was my job to lead them to a point where they can give a public speech to their friends and family in twelve week's time.

Often the turning point is on the second week when we went on a residential trip to a nearby activity centre. Having spent only one week meeting each other, now they are in a small cabin living with one another. It's not unusual that just the thought of leaving their home town would be fearful enough for some. Not long after arriving we are asking them to put on a harness in the middle of a forest and climb the 'leap of faith' - a thirty foot pole with a small platform with a trapeze bar two meters away hanging in the air.

We encouraged them to set themselves a target and go as high as they can. They would encourage each other and it was evident to see how proud they were for trying. After everyone had a turn, it was my go. *No problem*, I thought. After seeing a dozen of them climb the 30-foot pole and jump from the small platform, I figured it would be fine. The young people were very forgiving of each other and gave lots of encouragement, but now as a leader there was a certain expectation of me to 'perform'. I could feel the adrenaline beginning to flow.

The instructor tied the rope to my harness, I didn't take my eyes off the knot he was tying whilst he was speaking to me.

This knot was holding my life, literally. The knot was bigger than my fist so I assumed it would be okay. I approached the ladder that was precariously leaning against the pole and began my ascent. There were small foot and hand holes spaced every half metre. This bit was fairly easy and I began to see the platform above me. As I reached the top I took my first glance down and it was slightly higher than I anticipated. Keep going! I shouted in my head. I reached for the platform and began to pull myself over, feeling the instructor tugging on the rope to help me over. Now on my knees I was eye level with the trees around me. There was no banister to hold onto, just a one foot by three-foot-wide platform. What looked a reasonable size from the bottom, now seemed tiny beneath my feet. There was no room for error. I held onto the rope I was attached to pull myself up and find my balance.

As I stood up I could feel the whole platform begin to sway slightly with the wind. I made a mistake and looked down towards the others, trying to seem brave. In that moment a wave of fear rushed over like I'd never felt before. I felt so vulnerable. My brain was telling me, what are you doing up here?! As the fear pumped through my body, I could feel myself freezing - my body wanted to do anything other than jump. I knew the longer I waited the harder it would be to jump. Without thinking much more, I focused on the trapeze bar in front of me and counted myself down from three. Jumping as far as I could I grabbed the bar and smiled with relief towards the others below. As I spun around I grimaced towards the instructor telling him I was ready to come down.

Aside from my false bravery, I am always amazed to see the young people overcome their fears. These fears could be as small as attending each day, being in a room full of people or writing in a booklet, to helping support elderly people in the community. I would argue that all of them have overcome one of their fears by signing up for the course and attending on the first day. The majority of them would never had been able to stand in front of a group of 30 including their friends and family and deliver a speech after twelve weeks. But most of them do. It reminds me each day that overcoming fears is possible.

The most important thing to understand about fear is that there is rational fear and irrational fear. Rational fear is a survival mechanism that is designed to protect you. It's the feeling when you see a car heading towards you as you step into the road. It's also the kind of fear an animal senses when it is hunted by a predator. We respond with fight or flight, which is designed to save our lives. When I was standing on the small platform, my body wanted to leave because it sensed danger, but I knew I had to fight it in order to complete the task. I knew I had to step out of my comfort zone, make a calculated risk and overcome the fear.

Then there is irrational fear. This shows itself as worry and anxiety. This fear is believing all the things that could go wrong in an imaginary future. The scenario hasn't actually happened yet but we play out the options in our minds. I would argue that rational fear keeps us safe but irrational fear keeps us from living adventurously. Dr. Lissa Rankin, in her book, The Fear Cure, builds a comprehensive case that living with 'false' fear can affect your health, your effectiveness in your job, your interactions with others and most obviously your confidence.

Irrational fear might say to you, if you make that decision no one will love you, or, you are not good enough to try. This false fear often whispers to me that I am too young and have nothing to share. Fear might be telling you that you are silly for wanting to try something different from the norm, to retrain for a new job, to build different friendships or to move to a new city.

It is possible to overcome the barriers to fears but I don't want to attempt to write a self-help guide as there are many out there for combatting fear. But I would recommend a couple of things that I have learnt from others. Firstly, identify what you're scared of; flying, public speaking, water, intimacy with people, failure, commitment, spiders or needles (like me). Take time to acknowledge what holds you back from living with more purpose. Consider what it is holding you back from; trying new hobbies, joining a new group or having health relationships. Then reflect on where this fear comes from. For me, my fear of needles comes after fainting in hospital after having my BCG jab as a teenager. Most of our fears are rooted in something and it is imperative that we deal with the issue.

Secondly, surround yourself with friends who will support you. It is hard enough doing life alone, never mind overcoming fears by yourself. You need people around you who want the best for you. A friend once told me that good friendships are those who bring the best out in you. I hadn't see it that way before. It's a good measurement for a friend: do they like me as really am and do they promote the best in me?

My wife and I recently moved to a new area, not because of work or because of the home we live in but because of the people we live near. We prioritised being around a healthy

> It may be slow but find ways to befriend fear and overcome your barriers.

community of friends who can support us and people who we can invest our lives into.

Thirdly, as hard as it may seem, walk directly towards the fear. It may be slow but find ways to befriend fear and overcome your barriers. Be intentional about doing things that push you out of your comfort zone. This is a process of not letting letting your fears define or derail you. It is accepting they're present but not accepting that they'll stay for long. I forget which book I read it in, but it encouraged developing a relationship with fear. Sounds odd doesn't it? The author recommended purposefully saying, "Oh, hello fear", when anxiety suddenly builds up in you. Walking towards fear is choosing to not let your life be dominated by it. This isn't an overnight fix but will take years of building the resilience.

If this is all too much at once, just begin by acknowledging and identifying the fear. It may be helpful to share with a close friend so they can hold you accountable to the reflection you've done. For others it may help praying about the fear or even seeking counselling for it. I remember reading, "If you're brave enough to move gently and tenderly into your fear, you may find it loosening its grip on you, and slowly, like a seed sprouting, courage pushes through."

My friend Joe, who taught me to surf, noticed that I was terrified when a large wave was approaching because I always paddled towards the beach in the hope that I could escape the impact of the wave as it crashed down. His advice was, when I saw a large wave approaching, paddle towards it and not away from it. This was counter-intuitive for me. This was completely the opposite of what my mind was telling me to do. In life, when I saw something I feared I wanted to run away. Instead, Joe's advice was to confront it. If I paddled towards the wave I would increase my chances of getting over the top it before it crashed down on me.

In the same way, when you notice fear on the horizon, begin to make your way towards it. If you run away from it, it will only makes things worse. To ignore is to endure suffering but to confront is to overcome your giants. Adventurous living is learning what holds you back and why. Befriending your fears is living courageously.

Five

Facing Your Family

Charles Thomas Studd was driven to change the world and didn't allow anything to stop his pursuit. Money, health, age and distance from his family made no difference. Even his wife and two daughters did not stop him from travelling to Africa where he ate with cannibals, watched his house burn down and trekked through the jungle for days with simple supplies and a bicycle. Many missionaries consider C.T. Studd to have been foolish and irresponsible for leaving his family behind. Personally, I find his life encouraging whilst challenging.

I have found that understanding how our family influences how we make decisions is key to finding purpose for ourselves. The story that follows is an extreme example of pursuing our passions and not allowing family to be a barrier to adventurous living.

C.T. Studd, born in 1860, grew up in a wealthy and aspirational family as the youngest of three boys. At the age of eighteen, along with his older brothers, he was selected to play cricket for Cambridge University, much to the amusement of their father who said it would need more than three of them to make a great cricket team. C.T. was a young man who threw himself into any athletic challenge and was quickly asked to captain the Cambridge cricket team in 1879.

In that same year, C.T. was summoned into the headmasters office to be informed that his father had died. The last C.T. could remember was his father being healthy and fighting fit. Later his mother recounted the incident; Edward Studd planned to attend a meeting but had forgotten to his notes and decided that using a carriage would take too long to get home, so chose to run instead. C.T.'s father missed the meeting and was later found lying dead on the floor. It turned out he had burst a blood vessel in his leg and there was nothing the doctor could do. The family was thankful that Edward Studd had wrote clearly in his will how his fortune would be distributed. Each son would inherit a large sum of money (£29,000) on his twenty-sixth birthday and the oldest son, Kinny, inherited the family estate.

C.T. still struggling to process his father's death, continued to play cricket with his brothers and was recognised for his potential as a great cricketer. In matches the brothers made an unstoppable combination; in one match the three of them got 249 out of the 504 runs the Cambridge team scored. In 1882, the year when Australia made their third visit to England, the Aussie captain asked if they could play against the Cambridge eleven to the dismay of the Cambridge president. Australia had beaten every team they had played so far, what mockery it would be to play the Cambridge eleven! Despite the reservations of some, the team agreed and the match was scheduled.

After an exchange from both sides, it was C.T.'s turn to bat and scored fifteen runs not out, including the winning bat. Much to everyone's scepticism, Cambridge had done what no one thought they could do - they had beaten the formidable Australian cricket team. *Lillywhite's Cricket Record* concludes C.T.'s performance, "Very few players have a finer style: brilliant leg hitting and driving, with a very hard wrist stroke in front of the point, a real straight bat, and a resolute to nerve together a batsman whose back bowlers are very glad to see." Even though C.T. was only in his third year at college, he was ranked at the top of his sport. C.T. was surprised when asked to be a member of the English national team to play the next test match against Australia.

But once again C.T. was witnessing a member of his family approaching death's door. His older brother, George, had a bad case of pneumonia and there was little to be done to save him. C.T. spend hours at his brother's bedside, recounting stories and mountain top moments of beating Australia. *But what use are they to George now?* C.T. introspectively asked himself. *What is the point of spending your life chasing fame and wealth, when in the end you die and have to answer to God for the way you have lived? It could just as easily be me lying where George is now. What would happen if I were to die now? Where would I go?*

This was the turning point for C.T. Studd. Even though he had become a Christian six years before, his life had continued to revolve only around cricket. He had become the most famous cricket player of his time, but in this moment of contemplation, C.T. realised it seemed a silly thing to have spent his life pursuing. As he watched his dying brother, considering the reality of life, C.T. decided he would make more of his life than he had done already. He had a new set of priorities. On the third day at his brother's bed watched his brother open his eyes and grunt; this the arduous journey back from the brink of death

C.T. was grateful that his brother's life had been spared. Once hearing that Dwight Moody, an American Evangelical preacher was back in London he promised to himself he would hear Moody as soon as he could. In November 1983, C.T. attended a 'Moody meeting' and by the end of the evening he felt a fire in his soul. Something had changed in him. His heart overflowed with excitement. But now what would he do?

C.T. had enough money to make it to his twenty-sixth birthday where he would inherit enough to live comfortably for the rest of his life. As a result, he did not need to begin a career or enter the business world, instead his mind turned to the thousands of people who had never heard the gospel. C.T. resolved he would serve God and would try to change the world - but did not yet know how.

CIM (China Inland Mission) is an organisation set in the heart of China aiming to reach the unreached. In 1884, C.T. was invited to the CIM headquarters in London to hear a returning missionary from China. His name was John McCarthy. C.T.'s heart came alive as he heard the stories and adventures John told of travelling across China from Wuhan in the east to Burma in the west. By the end of the meeting he felt called to go. Just as C.T. suspected, his mother was horrified. His uncle accused him of breaking his mother's heart, and other family members begged him not to throw his life away. After all, he was from a family of status with a surplus of cash, surely this decision would effect the rest of the family. But C.T. was determined to live for his calling, no matter what it cost him in his family or public opinions. Little did he know how this attitude would shape his life.

In 1885, aged 24, C.T. boarded the ferry and squinted one last time to get a last view of his family as they became blurry dots in the distance. His dreams became realised as he arrived in China with a team of young men, full of vigour and zeal. The next challenge was to master the language and grow enough hair to make a pony-tail plait so he was able to blend into the culture as much as possible.

On C.T.'s 26th birthday, he received a letter confirming he had inherited the money that was promised to him. He had already planned to divide all of this money to charities and organisations and did so as soon as he could. Two years later in 1887, C.T. arrived back to the CIM guest house after a long trip to remote villages throughout China. It was here he met a women called Priscilla, whom at first sight appeared weak and frail, but after an evening conversation on the guest house porch, C.T. changed his mind.

Priscilla had a very similar up-bringing and was strong-willed and relentless, like himself. C.T. was overcome with excitement and later convinced Priscilla to marry him. Arrangements were quickly made and they both chose to dress in their usual Chinese attire. With little money to their name, Priscilla remembered she was previously given a ring which had the initials C.T.S engraved on the inside. Quite a coincidence! Their wedding vows promised to God and each other, "We will never hinder one another from serving God."

February 1889 saw the birth of their first child called Grace. Their cook, realising it was a girl, lingered around as the child was born. C.T. asked the cook why she spent so much time staring at the child.

"I was wondering if you intended to keep it, since it is a girl."

"What do you mean?" C.T. inquired, slightly off guard.

"Many mothers do not keep their daughters, especially if they don't have a boy already. There are certain places where mothers can leave a baby girl. The wolves can make quick work of them."

C.T. stunned and disgusted at the thought replied, "the Christian God tells us to value all life. Boys are no better than girls."

When Grace was one years old, Priscilla gave birth to another child who they named Paul. Unfortunately, Paul only lived a few hours and C.T. buried him in the corner of their courtyard. The living conditions in China, with minimal healthcare, were taking their toll on Priscilla and C.T. Over the years, the number in the Studd family had grown to four. C.T. was suffering from asthma because of the harsh climate and as a result his health was deteriorating. They decided to return to England. When he had left ten years before, he was a fit and healthy athletic young man, now he was returning in ill health, with a wife and four little girls who could not speak English!

C.T.'s time in England was one of frustration and refreshment. The young girls were now immersed in the upper-class English lifestyle and Priscilla was recovering from her own ill-health with the help of her mother-in-law. C.T. chose not to slow down and began preaching tours to share the trials and triumphs of China and to urge people to travel to China and join CIM. He often left his wife and children behind for months at a time. C.T. was unsettled in England and sought out his next adventure and learned that north India, which was situated in the hills had plantations accommodated for an easier climate. C.T. travelled to India alone with the understanding that when he found a suitable place, Priscilla and the girls would join. In October 1900, after finding a job as pastor of the Union Church in Ootacamund, the family joined their father. No sooner after they arrived did they realise the cool climate which attracted so many people was exactly the opposite climate that someone with asthma needed. It got so bad that Priscilla wrote home describing C.T. as a "wreck". In 1906, they returned home one more time. At the age of 46, C.T. asked himself if this would be the end of his missionary service.

Let's pause for a moment. It is quite easy to read about the life of Charles Thomas Studd and not think too much of it. But if you take a moment to put yourself in his shoes, there's something challenging about his decisions. When he first left his home for China, his family really did not approve of what he was doing, it is likely they did not grasp the bigger picture of what he was dreaming about.

C.T. had his mind set on greater things but his family had not.

C.T. had his mind set on greater things but his family had not. His father had earned status and wealth but to C.T. nothing compared to the needs in the third world. C.T. did not need affirmation and confirmation from his family to fulfil the call on his life. He was convinced about what he wanted to do, even if he wasn't able to communicate this with those he loved - instead he surrounded himself with those who understood.

But the worst was yet to come. C.T. now back in England began his preaching tours once again and one lunch time, walking down a main street of a city, he noticed in a building window a poster that read: *Cannibals want missionaries*. C.T. chuckled to himself but was interested to know more. He went inside the building to find Dr. Karl Kumm sharing his adventures of walking across Africa. C.T.'s heart came alive once more as he realised he needed to share the gospel in the heart of Africa. It did not matter that he was forty-eight years old, in poor health and had no money - he was convinced he had to go. Africa at this time was seen as an uninhabitable place to live, filled with deadly animals, challenging environments and an unbearable climate. Never mind the African natives who supposedly wanted to eat all white people.

C.T. went to Africa. On the trip C.T. sent letters home to Priscilla and his girls. He understood that this venture meant a huge sacrifice on her part and he hoped she would find excitement in what he thought was certain to be ahead of him. C.T. reflecting on his journey so far wrote to her:

> Somehow God tells me all my life has been a preparation for this coming ten years or more. It has been rough discipline. Oh, the agony of it! The asthma, what has not that meant, a daily and nightly dying! The bodily weakness! The being looked down upon by the world folk! The poverty! And have I not been tempted? Tempted to stop working for Christ! Doctors! Relatives! Family! Christians!

This extract gives us a glimpse into the frustration C.T. had. It seemed that everyone was trying to stop him from doing what he was called to do. No one believed in him. His family was convinced he was looking death in the face. But C.T. was unstirred. He later heard from Priscilla that she was unhappy living with her mother-in-law and he quickly made arrangements for Priscilla to move out into her own home.

The work C.T. pioneered in Africa is a recommended read on its own, as it speaks of his resilience and willingness to sacrifice his own life, family, marriage for the sake of those who had not heard the gospel. In 1913, C.T. ventured into the Congo; eating with 'the cannibals', building homes, carrying his bicycle, meeting indigenous tribes and trekking through the jungle. In 1926, C.T. had finally finished translating the New Testament and Psalms into the Kingwana language. Two years later, the mail cart brought a different type of cargo to Ibambi. When it stopped in the village, Priscilla Studd stepped out of it. She had not asked for the permission of C.T. and instead had told him when to expect her.

Many of the natives laughed and celebrated at the sight of Priscilla. They had heard C.T. had a white wife in England but many of them doubted if she actually existed. Now they were stood in Africa side by side. Priscilla had given her life serving in England so that the mission organisation they had founded would have enough missionaries and money to carry on its work. C.T. was taken back by how well she looked at sixty-four. Priscilla however kept her thoughts to herself at the appearance of C.T. With Priscilla now in the Congo, a series of meetings were arranged, allowing her to speak in the villages. However, she only spent two weeks with C.T. as the work in England called her home.

This time, when the couple parted, they knew it would be the last time they saw each other. From sharing their weddings vows many years before, they could have never imagined the journey and adventure life would take them on. From living in China, moving back to upper-class English culture, relocating to India and now standing on African soil. Their marriage was built on a deep friendship and promise that they would never "hinder one another from serving God". Slowly, arm-in-arm, C.T. walked Priscilla back to the mail cart. A crowd had gathered in silence as they said their farewells. C.T. watched Priscilla stepped into the cart, the door shut behind her and she looked straight ahead as the cart pulled away. C.T. felt that by her doing this, she was saying that they both had tasks to do and they need to keep their eyes on those tasks with all the strength they had.

In January 1929, Priscilla died after a single day's illness. She was C.T.'s last connection with England and he knew he would never return from the Congo. By 1931, C.T. was so ill that he seldom left his bed. C.T. lapsed in and out of consciousness and for every breath he fought, he uttered the word, "hallelujah." He died at the age of seventy.

There are no well-articulated words that can describe the life of Charles Thomas Studd. His life is a testimony that speaks about living an adventure despite all that life throws, especially family. C.T.'s family didn't want him to leave for China when he was 24 years old. Consider what would have (or not have) happened if C.T. gave into the fears, worries and concerns of his family. He loved his family dearly, but there was a greater call on his life and he was prepared to sacrifice a cosy English family lifestyle for the desire to change the world.

I do not advocate ignoring or abandoning your family. Family is a blessing we need to learn to appreciate more. However, I wonder how many times we allow our family to define who we are and what we do. Families can often be the barrier to adventurous living because they place expectations and hopes on us. I have mentored a handful of young adults who constantly sense the pressure of their parents to go to university or to do something 'normal' with their lives. To put it simply, some times our family can hold us back. Not out of bad intention, usually the opposite. They love us and they want to keep us close. But I wonder how our lives might look differently if we chose not to live under the expectation of our family?

For some, families aren't a barrier but a blessing. We need to use these close relationships to encourage and challenge us.

I'm thankful that my family have been encouraging towards me. Anything I chose to do, they thought it was amazing and took any opportunity to tell me, but they were also willing to challenge me. Many times they would ask, "have you thought of doing this?" or, "why don't you consider that?" Out of love, they challenged my thinking, actions and decisions. It's important to welcome encouragement and challenge from family.

But for others, families are often a barrier to living adventurously. They can hinder and restrain us. Families can distract us from our life's purpose because they don't want us to break out of the mould. To maintain healthy relationships, it can help to give your family plenty of notice before making big life decisions. Give them time to process any upcoming change. Ask what they think about your decision and discuss their worries and concern. Involving them in the decision may build your relationships over time.

For C.T. Studd, he chose not to live the predetermined comfortable life. Instead he focused his life on something he was passionate about. He gave himself to a greater cause. In the same way, your life can be an example to your loved ones as to what adventurous living looks like.

Six

Dancing With Resistance

When you say yes in life, you will face opposition. Plans don't often work out how you hope and they rarely work out at the right time. Facing opposition tests our strength, it examines our motives and refines our character. It's through those tough times when you begin to reassess if you are really passionate about your goals. Is it really worth the effort and heartache? The financial strain? Adventurous living is having the resilience, patience, integrity and courage to continue even when everyone else says it's not possible.

My time in Senegal, where I was volunteering for a year, was coming to an end and I began to consider my next adventure. A friend recommended I should study or train in something, as I hadn't been to university. I remember laughing to myself at the thought of studying again. I had not enjoyed school but as I grew older I discovered the joy of learning. The more I thought about it, the more I came around to the idea. I began to look for places around the world I could study. Just like when I was 17 after leaving my A Levels, I told my mother and she began searching with me. She came back with a list of options and I filtered through what I wasn't interested in and short-listed possible ideas.

One option could be to return to England and study at Redcliffe College that trained students to work overseas as missionaries. This meant three years of study and a lot of debt. I wasn't feeling too inspired. At the time I also learnt that WEC (World Evangelism for Christ) ran colleges around the world (Canada, Brazil, the Netherlands and New Zealand). The mission training courses are designed for people who feel called to work overseas in another culture. The colleges equip students with the skills and knowledge of how to understand and live in different cultures.

The course in the Netherlands began in September but I was finishing my voluntary time in Senegal in July, so I didn't feel it gave me enough time to rewind and raise financial support. I ruled out the option of studying in Brazil (because I would need to learn Portuguese) and the college in Canada was designed for short-term classes and not a year-long course. This left me with New Zealand that began in February, seven months away.

I returned to England to enjoy the temperamental summer and spent a few more weeks weighing up my options making sure I had covered all bases and kept asking myself, *"Luke, do you really want to study? You said you never would!"* It was now September and I decided I would apply for the college in New Zealand. I received a reply a week later saying I was accepted! I chose to take a risk and believe in myself.

Shortly after receiving the letter, I was sharing the good news with a friend as we walked back to my flat, he commented, "Being accepted isn't always a sign that you should go. Anyone can get accepted into these colleges." As I respected and looked up to him for the choices he had made, his opinion took the wind out of my sails. I tried to not to let it weigh me down.

The next step was to get the support from my church. I arranged to meet with the mission action team and presented my idea and plans. This team consisted of people who had been on their own mission trips in the past – one old chap had planted a church in the Amazon (who wouldn't let me forget about it) and the others had experience in short term trips.

I laid out my plan telling them I wanted study in New Zealand and presented the cost to them as well as how I planned to raise the finances. Do you know how some conversations don't go as well as you hoped? This was one of those. What I pictured in my mind was a response like, "Luke, what a fantastic idea, we think you're so brave, here's all the money you need. Send us a postcard when you arrive." Though more accurately it went something like, "Luke, do you realise how much this is going to cost? There are many colleges in England that do the same thing. Why do you want to travel half way around the world? Where will you find a sponsor for your visa?" Each time I took a step forward, it felt like I was met with resistance.

I left feeling deflated, but no less optimistic. I wouldn't give in without a fight. I realise it sounds a bit heroic, but I wasn't willing to give up this easily. One of my barriers was having a sponsor that had £7,500 in a savings account. The church could not act as my sponsor because they were listed as a charity, and since I was 22 years old I didn't have many friends with that much money lying around. The very same day I was visiting a friend and after explaining my predicament to my friend James, he calmly responded, "I can do that for you."

Frustrated by the conversations earlier in the day, I didn't take him seriously, "No you can't, don't be silly."

"Luke, I can do that for you."

"You have £7,500 lying around?"

"Sure."

"One, why on earth have you never told me this before? Two, can you print out a bank statement for me?"

To this day, my friend has always been a generous and humble man. The next day he handed over a bank statement. On Sunday I went to church and made small talk with friends as usual. I exchanged glances with someone on the mission action team and he smiled in acknowledgement. He held his gaze longer than the normal social etiquette requires which suggested he had something to say. I made my way over to him and told me directly, "Luke, we do not think it is right for you to go to New Zealand. I've talked with the others on the team and we can't enourage you because we do not think it's the right thing to do." I can't describe how punctured I felt by this. I joined my friends upstairs on the balcony and sat through the service feeling miserable.

The week after, wallowing in my misery, I met with an older friend I respected called John. It was a typical English day where it rains relentlessly. I met with John who was walking his dog, actually his daughter's dog (and to this day continues to complain about not wanting it) and I explained my situation. I had lots of questions, but John was wise enough to know I already had the answers, he just carefully teased them out of me. Whilst walking around the local park, getting drenched from head to toe, I told him the journey of feeling challenged by my friend in Senegal, how I had done the research about different options and colleges, how I sat on the idea for a month and how the mission action team had dismissed my plans.

Eventually, John timing his question carefully asked me, "Has your plan changed?"

"No." I replied, anticipating his next question.

"Do you still want to go?"

"Yes." I responded quickly but still confused.

"So, what is stopping you go?"

> Resistance can be a necessary part of the process because it makes you question how much you want something.

I didn't reply as quickly this time. Walking through the rain filled streets of Plymouth and despite the melancholic weather surrounding me, it was if someone flicked on a light switch inside. In contrast to the grey skies, inside I began to glow as the initial excitement and taste of adventure returned suddenly. I chuckled to myself having realised that I made my situation a bigger deal than it actually was. With a smile on my face, and looking down at my soaked trainers, I replied to John in a half laugh, "Well, actually nothing!"

Sometimes it takes a little encouragement from a friend to bring you back to your senses. Life will do everything it can to knock you off track and soak you through with doubt like the rain did to me on that day.

Whenever you have a dream or the taste of adventure, expect that someone will tell you can't. Expect opposition. Trust the guidance and wisdom of friends and family you trust, but learn to ignore those who don't want the best for you.

I asked to meet with the mission action team again and sat down with a confidence in the decision I had already made. Before they could say anything to me, I opened the discussion by saying that perhaps in the last meeting I may have sounded unsure about what I wanted to do, that it may have sounded more like I was trying to get them to fund a holiday. But actually, I was going in January whether they supported me or not. I told them I had already booked my flight tickets planning to visit my parents in South Korea and I had found someone to sponsor my visa.

I received an email a few days later saying they would support me in prayer and offered me £600 every quarter. That day I learnt persistence in opposition.

There are many famous stories of individuals who have overcome opposition, rejection and disappointment. Walt Disney was one of those. He began his career when he was fired by a newspaper for not begin creative enough. His 'Mickey Mouse' cartoons were rejected as they said to be too scary for women. More bizarrely, 'The Three Little Pigs' was also turned down because it didn't have four characters. Disney took many risks, hired different animators, created different characters and worked with different business partners. The golden age of animation came as Disney created 'Snow White and the Seven Dwarfs' which made $6.5 million in 1939, the most successful film at the time.

Nelson Mandela is a famous story for overcoming many trials. Despite the racial hierarchy in South Africa, he worked hard to train as a lawyer. Against the odds, Mandela was able to practice law, helping many black South Africans to survive in the apartheid system. Mandela was sent to prison for his opposition in the 1960's and yet he still played a crucial role in bringing equality to South Africa.

JK Rowling and her daughter were living on benefits whilst she wrote the story of Harry Potter in the cafes in Edinburgh. She had sent the script to twelve different publishers before someone saw the potential. After receiving numerous awards and writing many more novels, Harry Potter is a global brand and considered to be worth over £7 billion.

Bill Gates created something called the Traf-O-Data 8008, a device that could take traffic tapes and create useful data. He tried to sell the product but there was a fundamental flaw, it didn't work. Gates didn't give up and created Microsoft, today one of the biggest computer and software companies. Steve Jobs, another successful tech expert, faced opposition as he was sacked from the very own company he helped found. Jobs kept innovating and creating different products and even companies such as Pixar. He was later invited back to Apple which went onto create the most sought-after products of today.

Malala Yousafzai, a Pakistani school girl who openly ignored the threats of the Taliban to campaign for the right to education. She survived being shot in the head and has now become a global advocate for human rights, women's rights and the right to education. In 2011 she received Pakistan's first National Youth Peace Prize and finally after many campaigns and petitions she received The Nobel Peace Prize in 2014.

Don't get me wrong, I'm not associating myself with the heroes above who have changed history. My decision to go to New Zealand is insignificant in comparison. What I'm trying to highlight is how much these individuals had to go through to achieve what they did, their stories demonstrate what it is possible to accomplish despite opposition. These giants refused to say no amidst adversity.

Resistance can be a necessary part of the process because it makes you question how much you want something. When your decision is being challenged it can cause you to rethink how important it is to you. Opposition makes you reevaluate your plans and whilst it feels discouraging and disheartening it can often be more motivating.

Adventurous living is being resilient, patient and having the integrity and courage to dream big even when the people around you say it's not possible. It also begs to question of how to do conflict well. How to disagree healthily and how to challenge others. Margaret Heffernan (a CEO, entrepreneur and writer) explained in her TED Talk, *Dare To Disagree,* that it's actually important to surround ourselves with people who are different from ourselves. Generally speaking we surround ourselves with people who are similar to us, but we need to resist the echo chamber and seek out people who have a different background, upbringing and way of thinking.

I remember a friend telling me that you can only have an opinion when you understand both sides of the argument. It took me a moment to grasp this, but I still believe it's true.

Heffernan goes onto explain that generally we are too afraid of conflict. She explains that when we dare to break the silence and create conflict we enable ourselves and the people around us to do our very best thinking. To challenge others and to have constructive conflict requires us to be open and honest.

When you disagree with something in your workplace or feel there is conflict with a friend, the best place to start is with openness. By laying your cards down you are not concealing any hidden agenda. Experiencing opposition is a result of being honest because it is only when we dare to be honest we begin to address the things we care about.

Though there are times when we don't feel we are ready or want to challenge the system. Perhaps it's because there have been times in your life when you have been told you cannot do something or there have been times you've been told you're not good enough. Perhaps it's even those closest to you that say it's not possible. These incidences hugely impact our desire to make a difference in the world and we begin to settle for less.

Take time to reflect if your desire to live adventurously is being prevented because of the people around you. Have you begun to compromise for the sake of others? Perhaps it's appropriate to begin rethinking who you spend your time with and which of those people don't promote the best in you. It's time to start surrounding yourself with people who believe in you. This will drastically change your outlook on life.

Redefining your purpose is retaining integrity, despite what others are saying. Your plans or purpose may seem unmanageable or unrealistic. I would go as far as saying that if you're not being met with resistance, you're not dreaming big enough.

Often your plans will always make others feel uncomfortable. My hope is that you will no longer feel discouraged when you face opposition but it will build your resilience, focus and determination to achieve what you've set out to accomplish.

Part Two

Seven

Fighting Your Goliath

The dictionary defines courage as the mental or moral strength to venture, preserve, and withstand danger, fear or difficulty. Adventurous living is being courageous because it enables us to step out of our place of comfort and to face adversity. Courage is an inner strength that allows us stand firm when opposition surrounds us. As described in the story that follows, our physical size and strength don't define courage, but it's our determination and resolve to stay focused on the goals we've set, despite the giants that we're against.

The territory-seeking Philistines (in the 11th century BC), an ancient people usually known for their conflict, were camped in an area that belonged to the tribe of Judah. The Israelites were on the other side of the valley. Both armies were preparing for battle. Imagine a scene something like the Lord of the Rings where two armies are spread across the hill ridge, like human silhouette shapes, preparing for war.

The Philistines were a sophisticated people and advanced in their weaponry and some historians would argue they were a few generations ahead of the Israelites. Both armies would have been equipped with short-range weapons, swords, daggers and spears necessary for hand-to-hand combat. A section of the army would be armed with medium-range weapons that are designed to be thrown from a distance such as javelins because they were short and light. Behind the front row would be the long-range weapons, soldiers equipped with a bow for propelling arrows and other men responsible for the sling that was used to hurl stones.

Their armour was intended to protect the soldier's body as much as possible. The men would have worn a helmet, coats of mail and a breast plate as well as covering their shins. The foot soldier was required to carry a shield to cover any unprotected parts and it was customary to employ a shield-bearer who would carry the soldier's shield and weapons.

While the Philistines were waiting for the battle to commence, a man appeared from the camp, called Goliath. He wore a helmet of bronze and was covered in body armour weighing 54 kilos. His legs were covered in bronze armour and he carried a javelin strapped between his shoulders. In one hand Goliath held a spear, this alone weighing seven kilos. He was about seven to eight feet tall; terrifying to say the least. A shield-bearer led him down to the valley where Goliath began to shout to the Israelites on the other side, "Choose a man for yourselves and let him come down to me!"

It was a custom in those times for each army to select their best warrior to fight in a hand-to-hand combat on behalf of their army to avoid mass bloodshed. Goliath continued to bellow, "If he is able to fight with me and kill me, then we will be your servants! But if I prevail against him and kill him, then you will be our servants!"

The Israelites were terrified at the sight of this colossal specimen calling one of their soldiers to fight. For forty days Goliath fearlessly came out of his ranks, took his position and taunted the onlooking Israelites. But they didn't move.

Meanwhile, an Israelite called David was sent by his father to supply his older brothers on the front line with dry grain and loaves of bread. David was commissioned on a quest to deliver goods to his brothers and to attain a report to bring home to their father. David, being the youngest of his brothers, had the responsibility of tending to his father's sheep whilst his older brothers fought with the Israelites.

Sheep were an important commodity for the family as they represented wealth and were a means for trading, eating and in those times sacrificing. Any farmer will tell you that herding sheep is no easy task and David, in his young age, would have learnt the tricks of the trade for rounding up the flock.

As David was approaching the front lines to greet his brothers we can only guess what was going through his mind. David would have walked through the Israelite's camp seeing men helping each other put on their armour, men sharpening their swords, others tending to wounds and the smell of smouldering fires; the scenes of an army preparing for war. As David approached the camp of the Israelites they were preparing to go into battle.

Imagine the nerves, intimidation and adrenaline rushing through David as he hears thousands of men roar in unison. This environment would have been millions of miles away from his usual job of tending to the sheep at home.

Noticing that the armies were lining themselves up for battle, David dropped his possessions and ran to find his brothers on the front line. As he was talking with them, Goliath, like clockwork, came out of his ranks and shouted the same words as before. The men of Israel muttered to themselves, "Have you seen the man who has come up? They call him Goliath. Surely he has come to defeat Israel! The king will reward the man who kills him."

When Eliab, David's oldest brother, heard him speak to the men on the front line he rebuked him for leaving the sheep and for coming to the front line to see the action. David was having none of it. He continued to ask the men around him, "What will be done for the man who kills Goliath?"

Rumours began to spread that David had visited his brothers. David, gathering all the courage he had, went to speak with the king of the Israelites. "Don't worry about this Philistine," David told king Saul, "I will go and fight him." You can imagine king Saul's reaction as this shepherd boy is stood before him volunteering himself to go before all the soldiers. Saul replied, "Don't be ridiculous! You are not able to fight Goliath, you are only a boy. This man has been fighting since his youth."

David didn't step down. He recounted stories to king Saul of times, whilst taking care of his sheep, when bears and lions would try to steal them but he'd catch them and club them to death. "All right then, go ahead." Saul consented. He gave David his own armour and strapped a sword to him. David, now looking like a solider, took a few steps but realised he wasn't used to this extra weight.

David took them off and collect five smooth stones and put them into a bag. He grabbed his sling and headed over the valley towards the Philistines. Goliath, seeing someone approach, took his usual position. He sneered at David, "Come here, you are merely a young boy! All you have is stones!"

Without hesitation David approached Goliath, taking out his sling, flung a stone as hard as he could. It sank straight into Goliath forehead who fell to the ground.

Think for a moment how David's day turned out. He woke up assuming it would be an ordinary day. He probably washed, ate breakfast and tended to his flock. Although on that day, his father called him over and sent him on a mission to his brother who were camped with thousands of Israelites. This was David's first taste of battle and still he defeated the notorious Goliath. For David this was an ordinary day, little did he know that saying 'yes' would change his life forever. It can be the same for us. Saying yes to something today could affect the rest of your life. You just don't know.

There's something we can learn from Goliath also. Historians speculate that Goliath was humongous because he suffered from a disease called acromegaly which is caused by an overproduction of growth hormones. Effectively, Goliath was so big because he never stopped growing. As well as having abnormal size hands, feet and face, a symptom of the disease was poor eye sight. This could suggest why Goliath had the shield-bearer that would lead him down the mountain side, surely he would have been strong enough to carry his own weapons? Perhaps the shield-bearer led Goliath down because he couldn't see for himself where he was going. Also note that Goliath called David to come to him. If Goliath was so brave, wouldn't he have gone towards the tiny man appearing from the Israelite ranks? Perhaps it was because Goliath couldn't see David and needed him to come closer.

Essentially, Goliath's strength was his ultimate weakness. What made Goliath so strong was actually his downfall.

David didn't allow himself to view Goliath in the way everyone else did. David approached his challenge with confidence and courage. Goliath's size didn't deter David from the task at hand. He looked at Goliath with an alternative perspective, he looked past the size and power and was assured in his own capabilities to climb the mountain set before him. David used his experience in protecting his flock from bears and lions. He didn't know how to use king Saul's weapons, though he did know how to use stones to kill. David knew what he was good at and used this to his strength.

Consider how the story would look if David decided he needed to fight like a solider and went away for a month to train before he approached Goliath. Rather than meeting the status quo, David did what he was best at. He was confident in his abilities; though they were simple and feeble in the eyes of others. David had courage.

Whilst this is a story of courage and faith, it also speaks to our illogical assumptions about power. Generally speaking, we associate size with power. The bigger the tree, the stronger it is. The more muscles the boxer has, the harder he can hit. The larger the car engine, the faster it can go.

We all have Goliaths in our lives that can overbear us, dominate our thoughts and cloud our judgement.

More often than not, adventurous living is thwarted by a lack of courage to face our giants.

However, the Goliaths are only prominent in our lives because we allow them to be. Giants are scary but not invincible. Malcolm Gladwell notes in *David and Goliath*, "in reality, the very thing that gave the giant his size was also the source of his greatest weakness." Essentially the powerful and strong are not always what they seem.

The commitment to a relationship or marriage; applying for that job that you know would make you happier but pays you less; asking for forgiveness or equally forgiving someone who hurt you. Confessing a weakness to those closest to you; doing something about the guilt you feel when you see poverty in the world; challenging your boss to think more compassionately. Taking the first step in a project you dream about; allowing yourself to be vulnerable despite the fear of attack and critique. Travelling overseas; speaking to someone you don't know; going back to University or college to study; telling that person your feelings and overcoming the worry of not being able to provide for your family are all examples of Goliaths in our lives.

From a distant horizon, our safe place, we see this intimidating concept shouting to us, "Come down and fight me!" This is the last thing we want to do!

However, not doing anything pins us down. Like the Israelites were in their camp; they made no progress in the battle. The same can be for us when we allow our giants to overwhelm us, we make no progress in life. Unless we overcome these barriers we won't live adventurously. More often than not, adventurous living is thwarted by a lack of courage to face our giants.

A giant faced in was 1800's was the slave trade. William Wilberforce was born in 1759 in Hull to the son of a wealthy merchant. While studying at Cambridge University he made friends with the future prime minister. In 1780, he became a member of parliament and when he became a Christian in 1790 he became interested in social reform.

Wilberforce spent his life campaigning for the end of the slave trade which, at the time, were carrying black slaves from Africa to the West Indies in unbearable conditions. For 18 years, Wilberforce tried to convince parliament for motions against the slave trade. For 18 years he consistently showed up at parliament. Finally, in 1807, Wilberforce conquered his giant and the slave trade was abolished, though it wasn't until 1833 that the act was passed and freedom was given to slaves in Britain. It was courage and determination that enabled

Wilberforce to stand in Parliament and stand firm for what he believed in.

Adventurous living requires us to first identify our giants. Perhaps it's a social issues, like it was for William Wilberforce, or it could be financial debt, family issues, self-confidence, mental health or decision making. By identifying our giants, we know what we are facing. It can require an honest self reflection to acknowledge the things we're scared of addressing. You can do this by spending time journaling or talking with a friend to answer the questions, what is holding me back? What worries do I have that I'm not dealing with? What are the fears that are consuming my thoughts?

Secondly, we need to replace the lie we believe about our giants with the truth. For example, if you feel like you are not good enough, the truth is that you are more than capable and you do have the confidence. If the lie you believe is that you are a failure, the truth is that regardless of previous experience you can succeed with the right motivations and hard work. If you feel you don't deserve to be loved, the truth is you likely already have friends and family who love you just are you are.

Whilst the giant feels very real and at times unmanageable, it's important to remember that giants aren't always as big as they seem. Like David slowly approaching Goliath, so you can begin approaching your giants and begin to see that the mountain ahead is more achievable than you originally thought.

Courage is the inner strength to begin your venture and preserve through the fear or difficulty. Adventurous living is underpinned by courage because redefining your purpose isn't always easy. It's an intentional decision to approach life alternatively by not living under the lies you have believed. Throughout life there will be many challenges along the way but they won't defeat you if you choose to live courageously.

Eight

Say Yes To Opportunities

After two years of studying music technology and sound engineering I was now 19 and decided to get more involved in my local church in Plymouth. I joined a pilot internship program where we would participate with the various groups run by the church. Shortly after starting the internship I discovered that a couple of friends from the church, Joe and Becky, were leading a trip to Madagascar where Becky had grown up with her missionary parents. This would take place the following summer. The short-term trip was aimed at students to give them an opportunity for adventure through their summer break. Joe asked if I'd like to go to make up the numbers for the men even though I wasn't technically a student. A six-week trip to Madagascar, that didn't sound a bad idea, so I said yes. Adventure first, worry later. I had a year to save for the flight tickets.

Just six-months later in March, my Dad asked me if I'd like to join a trip to Italy for two weeks, helping out in a rehab community called Betel. We wouldn't be helping with the rehabilitation side of things because there was a language barrier and Betel are against volunteers coming into their home and telling the men 'what they should do.' Instead, we would spend the two weeks doing maintenance on the house and helping out where the full-time staff did not have time.

I was asked if I'd like to join because they were short of people for the trip to be cost-effective. It cost £350 with flight tickets. I couldn't afford that. I put an application form into my church's mission action team and they gave me £250 – things started to look promising. I pulled together another £100 and joined the team a few weeks later.

The guy who ran the short-term mission trips at the time was called Brian. I met him when I did a team briefing for the trip to Italy, little did I realise how he would put me in a position that would change my life. The trip to Italy was amazing. It would be difficult to try and describe in a few sentences. The highlight was cleaning their swimming pool and painting it so the residents and their families could use it over the summer.

I don't think I've ever sweated so much as I did when I was brushing the walls of the pool in 30 degree heat. I now know what being in an oven feels like. After cleaning the pool thoroughly, we began to paint it with a special water-based acrylic that had been purchased by the house leader.

I should explain that Betel is an organisation that lives by faith meaning they are not like a charities that request for money or are funded by a larger pool of money, but they are self-sustainable. They receive food from local supermarkets and the men, who are healthy enough to work, run a furniture shop where they renovate furniture and sell it on again. This money alone has to support 20-30 men and all the running cost of maintaining the house. As you'd imagine, buying paint wasn't at the top of their list!

When you paint a swimming pool, I can speak from experience now, you need a thick coat of paint because you are not only painting the walls but also protecting the walls from being damaged from the chlorine in the water. After sending the house leader out a few more times to buy us more paint (we were surprised how much we needed), eventually he told us there wasn't any money left. We were 90% finished and just the steps remained with very little paint left. Like any good Christian mission trip, in a time of need, we gathered together and prayed. I've prayed for many things, but this has been the only time I've prayed for paint. To our surprise (even though we had prayed) we continued with the little we had and found there was enough!

We filled up the pool and invited the whole Betel community and their families to enjoy the pool on a warm Sunday afternoon. There's nothing quite like sweating buckets, working for hours painting eight-foot walls then seeing the hard work being enjoyed by those who had recovered from their addictions.

This trip left me on a spiritual and emotional high and whilst challenging, it gave me another taste for adventure. I couldn't wait for the trip to Madagascar! My internship year was coming to an end and I needed to make a decision about what I'd do afterwards. I searched around for different jobs and possible oversees trips but I was in a time of life where I didn't really know what I wanted from life. I didn't want to make any big commitments or find myself stuck in a job. At 20 years old, I wasn't interested in a career and I certainly was not interested in going to University.

My first trip oversees was volunteering with a project where we rebuilt small homes in the slums in Mexico. Now I had also experienced adventures in Italy, along with the

Madagascar trip coming up, I knew there was more I could see and do. I wanted to continue the momentum of not remaining in my comfort zone and I wanted to continue challenging myself.

When making a decision, there is a tendency to worry about what friends and family are doing, perhaps their job or where they live. This is understandable as we look to our family and friends for guidance and influence. However, too often we compare ourselves against them and measure ourselves up to make sure our lives don't look too abnormal.

It's a dangerous mindset to have. Imagine your life as a running track with two lines outlining your lane whilst being next to a bunch of other runners. If you compare yourself with them or worry about what they are doing, effectively you are running with your head looking to the left and right watching them. Have you ever tried to running with your head to the side looking around? I wouldn't recommend trying and I'm sure it doesn't work. Neither does comparing your journey with others. Unless you're looking forward, it's unlikely you'll get anywhere at all. It becomes a barrier to adventurous living because you become concerned about what people will think of you.

It was two weeks before I went to Madagascar. I was in my room with ideas circling around my mind. *Brian.* I opened up my laptop and googled WEC International and found, under the link of WEC Trek, Brian's number. I gave him a call.

"Brian, I'm sort of coming towards the end of an internship thing I'm doing, and I – enjoyed the trip to Italy… and was wondering if there's anything else I could do or help with?" Here's a little bit of advice. Be careful what you ask when you call a mission organisation. I know now, but I didn't then, they always need help.

Brian replied, "Hi Luke, yes, glad you enjoyed the trip. Well… we have a few things you could do. You can join us here in London and do a year working at the headquarters, or – there's a mission school out in Brazil that are looking for help, though their situation is quite unstable so I'm not sure about that. Or… there's a school in Senegal that need staff for the new school year."

Not knowing where Senegal was, I replied, "Senegal sounds great, what would I do at the school?"

He explained there are a variety of roles from teaching, cooking and helping in their dorms. Helping in a school? I hated school. Surely I didn't want to voluntarily spend a year in a school. I told Brian I'd think about it and call him back. A week later Brian called me. "Luke, I know you're going away soon and we need an answer if you'd like to go to Senegal?"

> It may open your eyes to seeing things in a different way. It could even awaken a passion you didn't know was there.

Do you know that feeling when you haven't quite made up your mind on something? Within seconds my mind listed, like a matrix of numbers, the positive and negative things about going. In that moment all I could think about was money. How would I have enough money to pay for all this? I had just spent a year saving for a trip to Madagascar, what was I thinking of signing up for a year in West Africa?! My mind thought back to a friend called Ben who once said to me, "God's will, God's bill." I'm not sure how theologically correct this is, but for me it didn't matter. I figured there would be a way of making it work out. I said yes to Brian, hung up the phone and began packing my bags to visit Madagascar, the tropical island that I'd seen David Attenborough talk so much about.

Decisions are hard to make. A mixture of common sense and culture teaches us to think; but what if? What if I don't have the money? What if people think I'm stupid? What if it doesn't work out?

We allow the negatives to outweigh the positives. This is because we can entertain the negatives in our head and see ourselves not having enough money to pay for the flight tickets or packing our bags to return home. We can see ourselves having to reapply for jobs or even having to explain to our family and friends that it didn't work out. The problem with this is we don't allow ourselves to foresee the positives that may happen. On the trip overseas, in the new job or the group you would help in, how do you know it won't change your life forever? You could meet some amazing friends, discover a career you hadn't considered or learn some skills that will help you in the future. It may open your eyes to seeing things in a different way. It could even awaken a passion you didn't know was there.

If it's the only option then it's the only decision. Tim Ferris in *The 4-Hour Work Week,* promotes the school of thought that if you fully commit yourself to something, like quitting your job to go travelling, it forces you to sink or swim. When you throw yourself into something, it's likely you'll find yourself swimming even though initially you thought the challenge would be too hard or even impossible. When I was involved in church youth work and quit after four months, I handed in my resignation without another job lined up. Against common sense, I just knew it was the right decision. This forced me to find work as I had no other option! Fortunately, it worked out and I had a new job by the end of the month.

Procrastinating and thinking, "it can wait for tomorrow" won't serve you well if you want to live adventurously. When I bought my first car and was unsure if I should go through with it, the salesman said, "A car today is gone tomorrow." Meaning if I didn't make the decision to purchase the car now, it's likely someone else will buy it tomorrow. Aside from it being a clever sales tactic, there's truth in putting off decisions because it may mean it's not available tomorrow.

I'm not suggesting you should rush decision making or be incredibly impulsive, but what I'm promoting is making the most of opportunities when they come up.

What's important is that we make good decisions and whilst family and friends can be a barrier they can also provide invaluable support. It's vital that you ask what your closest friends think is best for you. Spend time meeting with those you trust and map out your plans with their advice and suggestions. Remember you may be met with opposition, as we've discussed, though hopefully if your friends are wanting the best for you, they will challenge and encourage you.

Additionally, play out the scenarios in your head, which option makes you happiest further along the road? Consider which option has the most meaning and purpose, not necessarily the quickest fix or what makes most sense. When deciding on material purchases, try to divide them between *needs* and *wants*. *Needs* are those things that are necessary and essential whereas *wants* are those things that can wait a month or two. When making longer term decisions and weighing up careers, travelling, locations and friendships; ask yourself what will make you most fulfilled. Which option will give you the best memories? Which options feels more adventurous and risky?

Making decisions is like a muscle, the more we exercise the easier it will get. Saying yes to the small decisions each day makes it easier to saying yes to the larger ones when they arise. It would have been unlikely that I would have said yes to a year in Senegal if I hadn't continued to say yes to the smaller adventures that were presented to me. Begin to consider if there are opportunities around you at the moment that you can say yes to. Are there any offers you've missed recently that you can learn from? Always remember when making decisions about opportunities, even if it feels big or small, you have no idea where it may take you.

Nine

Say No To Tango

A friend whilst giving me a lift, caught wind that it was my birthday soon. We made the usual jokes about getting old (as he is a few years older than I am) and I asked what he has learnt from life. He pondered for a moment as we drove. "Learn to say no," he said. "You're a kind guy Luke, but learn to say no to people because they'll want to walk over you." I replied with a grunt of understanding as I processed his wisdom. It's a simple point he was making. Don't be pushed over by people who want to use your generosity and willingness for their own benefit. He was encouraging me to know my own boundaries and limits. Without these limitations it's difficult to know when to say no.

I have come across this situation since the conversation and I also noticed it in close friends who would ask me favours because they didn't want to do something themselves. They would assume that I would be willing to drop everything I was doing just to do a menial job they couldn't be bothered to do. Saying no requires us to carefully define our boundaries to protect us from being used and abused. You may find when you say yes frequently, people will assume you are always willing and they will keep asking many things from you. This will become burdensome and quench your spirit of adventure. The key is learning the right things to say yes to.

I learnt this lesson when past work colleague asked me if I wanted to join her at a Tango class. She gave me a month to decide. Trying to live out this philosophy of saying yes, I said yes to her, half hoping that it would be cancelled. I mean, I'm sure Tango is fun for some, but I really didn't think it was for me. She kept reminding me that we were going to Tango, but I still had reservations. Over a coffee she tried to convince me that I would enjoy it, she said that everyone that goes is friendly and it's suitable for beginners. I still wasn't won over by the idea and said I would think about it. My mind was already made up, I knew I didn't want to go. I questioned myself, *is it just fear of looking silly? Is it worry of dancing with someone from work? Am I just being lazy?*

Whilst my feelings were legitimate, I didn't want to force myself into doing something I didn't want to do just to please someone else. I knew from the start that I didn't really want to go to Tango. Dancing isn't my thing. I examined my motives and reasons for not wanting to go and I resolved that it was okay to say no. I called my friend and apologised for getting her hopes up. I explained that I needed to be honest with myself because I knew I wouldn't enjoy it. I told her it wasn't anything personal and there's lots of fun things we could do to hang out - Tango just wouldn't be one of them! It wasn't the fear of going to a new group and potentially making a fool of myself, it was just Tango. I knew it was no.

It's important to know when to say no and when to say yes. You are not doing yourself any favours if you continue to pressure yourself into doing something you don't enjoy. I don't like spicy food. I won't eat a vindaloo in the hope that I will love it. However, this mindset doesn't justify doing things you haven't tried or are merely worried about. The whole point of saying yes is to try new things. Of course it's okay to dislike something and say no the next time. This is the process of discernment and discovering life.

In *Making Of A Leader* by J. Robert Clinton, he researches that those aged 1-20 are in the fundamental learning stage. At this age they soak in everything around them and say yes to everything because they learn by experience. 20-30 year-olds say yes to most things but not everything because when they are in the second stage of learning where they discover there are things they don't like doing. They also begin to find those things they really enjoy and start doing them more. 20-30's begin to narrow their yes to things they enjoy doing and gives them purpose. At this age there is a pressure from society to find that single 'yes' (a job, a career, a relationship), but more often than not it doesn't happen overnight.

Clinton goes on to explain that 30-40 year-olds begin to say no more often than yes because they have decided what they want to do and can narrow their purpose to a few things. They know what makes them happy and don't feel the need to say yes to everything. Broadly speaking, 50-70 year-olds are considered at the optimal stage for being efficient and effective with their yes. Those in their 50-70's are strict with their no's and can clearly define their yes. At this stage they have discerned what they should and shouldn't be doing with their lives. They have directed their attention into a handful of things and become a master of it.

This doesn't mean we should wait until our 50's before we begin to say no to things or have a clear idea of how we will live with purpose. But for the 20-30 year-olds it's important to realise that whilst yes can lead to adventurous journeys, saying no is just as crucial. Saying no can protect you from burnout, being over worked, from being too busy and from having too much on your plate to focus on doing a few things well. Saying no is protecting your boundaries.

We are at risk of burning out when we say yes too often and have not learnt to say no. Burnout is a result of not being in control of your daily demands, when you are not working towards the goals that motivate you and when you lack the social support. All of which are affected by other issues like finances, family, responsibilities, employment and countless more. As a result, life becomes imbalanced and to prevent this, we need healthy boundaries.

These boundaries need a framework, physically and emotionally so we are able to engage with all aspects of life. Boundaries are healthy limits we set between ourselves and other people. They define who we are and who we are not, what we are comfortable with and what we are not. It's important to consider that boundaries are not just for relationships (although fundamental) but also healthy to have boundaries for areas such as work, volunteering, alone time and socialising.

One of my boundaries is that I view my working hours as strictly 9am to 5pm. Since I am contracted to work 37.5 hours a week, I try to keep within those boundaries and not allow the responsibility of work to spill into other areas of my life. I find this to be a healthy boundary because it helps me switch off from work and gives me a time-frame each day for when I should be thinking about work. It's also helpful in my friendships with colleagues because they know I'll be aiming to leave at 5pm. I've come to realise that having a clearly defined boundary with work helps me to say no. This clear boundary helps me keeps a good work-life balance. When life becomes imbalanced, that's when stress, anxiety and burnout begin to emerge. Without boundaries, people (even our friends and family) can treat us in any way they like.

When you are struggling to say no, how can you bring clarity to your boundaries, to the goals you've set and to re-ignite the fire for the things you're passion about? Our well-being needs constant attention and daily assessing to ensure we are healthy. The 5 commonly known 'ways to wellbeing' is a good foundation for having healthy and focused life.

1) Connect. Feeling close to someone and being valued by them is a fundamental human need. Social relationships are a must for good wellbeing (in real life, not on social media).

2) Be active. Studies show that regular physical activity help to reduce depression and anxiety. Find a way of staying active in a way you enjoy. This doesn't necessarily mean joining a gym but it could mean walking regularly with a friend, joining the National Trust and exploring woodlands or using the helpful apps like Couch To 5K to give you motivation and clear goals.

3) Take notice. This is being aware and being present. Notice the beauty around you and savour those moments. Be intentional in taking time away from your normal schedule and get away to the country or coastline to take a pause.

4) Learn. Continuing to grow in your understanding about life will also improve your self-esteem and your social interactions. Learning can start small or mean retraining in something you care about.

5) Give. Find ways to give your time, money and resources to those around you who are in need. You will find it incredibly rewarding knowing you have helped someone.

When you have healthy boundaries and feel good with your well-being, you will find it much easier to say no. Adventurous living is taking care of yourself. It is just as much about being as it is doing. When you take care of yourself, physically and emotionally you will find more joy to life. You get one shot at this, so why not be prudent and use boundaries to protect yourself from what is unhealthy so that you are able to pursue your passions and life adventurously? In his book, *Happiness by Design*, Paul Dolan writes, "You will be the happiest you can be when you allocate your attention as best as you can."

Tobias Jones, in his book *A Place of Refuge*, writes about his experience of communal living where he chose to move his family to a litter-filled former quarry in Somerset to test a new way of life. The aim was to live self-sustainably by growing their own food and building their own home. Their house, Windsor Hill Wood, is a project with no rules, no experience and no legal structure where people would live with them and guests would contribute to the community. Driven by the desire to return to the roots of interaction with individuals from all walks of life, Tobias opens his home to whoever visits. He shares his food, his resources, his skills and most preciously, his family.

Whilst living in the woods as a community with strangers might sound a romantic way to live authentically, it was messy and chaotic to say the least. There was an endless stream of people passing by, looking for connection, for work, for family or just for a place to sleep. Tobias recalls one time there being a girl called Hayley, a recovering addict who smelt so bad it was difficult to eat in the same room as her. There was also Ben was a guy who spent his time looking only at porn magazines. Then there's Chloe, a teenager with anorexia who self-harms and has OCD. Also Darren, a former solider with panic attacks at the slightest noise.

Consider sharing your home and meal times with people you don't know. Over time, Tobias began to see a change in the people he opened his life to. Of course, there were many people who wouldn't cooperate with community life and left.

But those who did stay began to find purpose with their daily tasks of cleaning the pigs or tending to the vegetables. Their personalities also altered as they became more generous and loving towards each other. But with an open-door policy, it wasn't long before Tobias experienced compassion fatigue and it all became too much.

> "You will be the happiest you can be when you allocate your attention as best as you can."
>
> Paul Dolan, *Happiness by Design*

There were many people who were manipulative and began to walk through his family telling him what he should and shouldn't be doing. One day it was too much for Tobias as he realised these guests were playing with his kids more than he was.

In the early years of the project, Tobias had unclear boundaries. Guests didn't know what was expected and assumed they could do whatever they wanted. Tobias writes about how some individuals even moved items around in his kitchen to make themselves feel more at home. He knew he had to enforce boundaries, to decide to say no to protect his wellbeing and his family. Tobais began to add rules such as everyone returning to their rooms before 9pm so he could spend time with his family. Also everyone had to contribute the same amount into a communal purse that purchased all the food and resources. There were set times for dinner and a rota for who would cook and who would wash up. They had regular meetings to decide the tasks for the day and met together afterwards to debrief how it went. It was only through these boundaries that Tobias began to find order amidst the chaos.

There's a verse in the Bible that says we need to guard our hearts and minds. Life tries to throw things at you to distract and tempt you; wealth, love, status and materialism to name just a few. Saying no is having the wisdom to know what is superficial and the discernment to pursue the things in life that are meaningful and lasting. The writer in this Bible passage tells us to guard our metaphorical 'heart' because this is where our values, passions and desires belong. Whilst also guarding our 'mind' as this is where we hold truth and reasoning. Saying no is placing boundaries around those things which you know are true and not allowing the world to tell you otherwise.

But, what should we say yes to? I would recommend measuring it against what makes you happy and what gives you purpose. Once you've decided on those two things, say yes to what comes your way and say no to those things that don't line up with it. If someone invites you to Tango and you don't want to go, then definitely say no!

Ten

The Beauty Within

One of the most fundamental ways to get the most out of life is to readjust the way we view people. How we view one another and how we project ourselves will massively contribute towards how we redefine what living with purpose means. Seeing people in a better way is giving ourselves permission to not 'judge the book by it's cover' but to look below the surface. When we allow ourselves to view people as they are, we begin to see the beauty inside one another. As I will discuss, this requires vulnerability and authenticity on our part. As we begin to refocus our lens we realise we actually need each other and to connect with one another we will need community.

When I first moved to Brighton I was inspired with how creative and fun the city appeared. Brightonians have a quirky fashion, love street art and drinking cortardo's (unnecessarily small coffee). I made attempts to blend in only to quickly realise how shallow my friendships were. Whether it was the culture of Brighton or the people I met (possibly a combination of both), what I desperately craved was depth to my friendships. I wanted to share life with people and not just be tagged in their online posts. After living in Brighton for a few years I learnt the importance of nurturing genuine relationships. It was hard not to be sucked into the surface level lifestyle and in many ways it forced me to pursue exactly the opposite.

I learnt that true love is vulnerable love. We cannot experience a depth in love until we learn to be vulnerable with one another. Many of us desire love but aren't willing to be vulnerable. To be vulnerable is not to seek a false affirmation but rather an authenticity in our relationships with those around us. As technology multiplies (yet weakens our friendships) there is a compelling desire for us to relearn the intricacy and tangible intimacy of relationships. There is beauty in each of us, we just need to readjust our lens to see it.

To define beauty would be to combine qualities such as shape, colour and form that are aesthetically pleasing to look at. We are hardwired to recognise beauty and innately have a desire to connect with it. Often when we talk of beauty, we think of a face. Studies show that as children grow up they build an emotional connection with facial recognition and therefore still associate an emotional connection with the facial features they prefer. Researchers argue that symmetry and balance in proportion is essential for the definition for beauty. Let's consider how has this affected our culture today. As our association with beauty has evolved, so has our prejudice with what we assume is *ugly*. Research has shown that those who categorise themselves as looking ugly also feel ugly inside.

James Partridge was driving to Oxford when he was 18 years old but didn't complete the journey. Whilst driving he tragically crashed and caught on fire but narrowly escaped. James Partridge underwent facial reconstructive surgery for five years. Afterwards he said, "It's no longer a medical issue, as much as it is an emotional and social issue. I've had to learn how to walk down the street." James Partridge went on to pioneer an organisation called Changing Faces that reaches out to those with facial differences.

There is beauty in each of us, we just need to readjust our lens to see it.

A person's beauty is not surface level and their beauty is not always on display. It's a takes a conversation and a friendship to truly appreciate the inner-beauty of a person. We need to remove our judgement about who we think people are and allow ourselves to truly get to know them. We have become shallow in disassociating ourselves with people we don't want to be seen with just because of the way they look.

Jean Vanier, a philosopher and Catholic social innovator began the L'Arche movement that centres around people living with mental disabilities. His insight into the lives of people who are overlooked and unwanted is profound and humbling. "What touches me the most about people suffering from disabilities is their cry for relationships. They had lived in psychiatric hospitals for many years and experience a lot of rejection."

Jean Vanier notes that Jesus, at the end of John's Gospel, asks his disciple the question, "Do you love me?" To parallel this to our lives today we ask the same question (although unlike Jesus our reasoning is purely focused on ourselves) through our social media posts and our inaccurate photos begs the indirect question to our friends, "do you love me?".

We are each created so wonderfully and yet we are fragile. Jean Vanier continues to explain that "our deepest desire is to be appreciated." We seek to be valued, to be wanted, to be acknowledged and to be loved. We are frightened by people who are different from ourselves, disfigured or disabled because it forces us to confront reality. And yet paradoxically, on the other end of the spectrum, we are threatened by those who are more beautiful than ourselves. We have a contorted lens through which we view humanity. CS Lewis in *Mere Christianity* wisely said, "Our experience is coloured through and through by books and plays and the cinema, and it takes patience and skills to disentangle the things we have really learned from life for ourselves."

I am convinced that if we spend more time searching for the beauty inside one another, rather than falsely projecting ourselves, we will begin to find more meaning to life. If we intentionally stop for a moment, a temporary pause from the hectic world, we are able marvel at what human beings are. We have the ability to create, to give and receive love. We hold memories, we push ourselves to new limits and we can even communicate with our eyes alone. We can empathise with hurt and we can feel euphoria where we are excited. Our bodies can heal themselves and our brains are deeply complex. Some people love to learn, many are still learning to live and the key to an adventurous life is living to love.

As humans we are designed to interact with one another. From the beginning of time, we shared a common union with one another and decided if we were to survive on this wonderful planet we ought to get along and cooperate. Another word for this inbuilt wiring is community. We all desire and seek community in one way or another as we aren't supposed to be alone. People gravitate to others who share common interests. It might be golf, swimming, rock music, sky diving, watching comedy shows, going to church or reading books. It's unlikely you will choose to a build friendships with someone if there's no common ground.

A community when it is functioning healthily is a fulfilling place to be. A community could be a friendship group, a family, a work place or a volunteer team. In a community everyone works together for the sake of the common goal. A person cannot be selfish or refuse to communicate; this would result in an unhealthy community. To live in common-union is to seek the needs of others first; to consider your own wants and desires second to that of your friend.

It's important to think about what community looks like for you because as our culture is advertised as being 'more connected', we are actually being pulled further apart. The way you interact with people within your community can affect the way you relate to life itself. If you make life just about yourself, it's unlikely it will be adventurous. But if you decide to live your life for a bigger cause, within a community, you'll experience a deeper meaning and purpose to living.

A healthy community is rarely made up on the same type of people. Within the communities you are likely to find introverts or extroverts. Introverts fuel their energy by spending time on their own, or with a few select people. They are not necessarily the quietest people in a social group, but they often need alone time so they can recharge their batteries. Introverts tend to be the deeper thinkers as they are usually introspective and soul searchers.

Extroverts however get their energy from being around people and avoid isolated time on their own. Not because they don't like being on their own but because they simply enjoy the company of other people. Extroverts are fun to be around because they know how to keep the energy in a social situation going. Extroverts are doers and not necessarily thinkers and are the first to try new things without overcomplicating. It is likely your friendship group is a compilation of extroverts and introverts and it is likely there is a common interest that threads you all together. Make sure you value all types of personalities as everyone has something valuable to contribute.

However, whilst this sounds great, it's not always how we experience the world today. Everyone has their own agendas and plans for success. Some of your friends may appear to be companions on the surface but really it's because they want something from you. Many people have hundreds of friends on social media but no one to spend time with on the weekend. Many people crave community and so exchange their integrity and common sense for a compromised lifestyle. Whilst social media has increased our communication with one another, it has decreased our ability to actually communicate in person. It's now easier to send a friend an emoji via a text than actually look them in their eyes when they need you.

Why is it normal to have a social media profile about ourselves? It's actually more strange to not have one. Our culture is increasingly becoming narcissistic. Most of us realise the tragedy of how this is affecting us, but the further we try to run away from it, the deeper it pulls us in. We irrationally delete our social media accounts because it's frustrating, but the thought of what everyone is doing and what we're missing out on begins to eat away at us. Because we can't see a friend's latest photo, we wonder who they are spending time with. Whilst we all seek community and deep friendships, we are often looking for it in the wrong places and going about it the wrong way. Social media serves a purpose, but if you allow it to become the basis of a friendship, you've missed the whole point.

Alongside community we need vulnerability. The word vulnerability suggests weakness. And that's exactly what it is. It's being weak with one another. Our natural tendency is to run as far as we can from being vulnerable because we don't know how to be weak with each other. The Oxford dictionary defines being vulnerable as: in need of special care, support, protection because of age, disability, or risk of abuse and neglect. Aren't we all in need of care, support and protection? I know I am. I need emotional care, support and protection. That's normal.

If we view the trends in our culture today we begin to see a resistance to weakness. We don't know what to do with our weaknesses, so we hide it and pretend it doesn't exist. When we don't know how to deal with our weaknesses, we certainly won't know what to do with other people's weaknesses. This results in a culture where you reply to the question, how are you? With, "I'm fine." Nine times out of ten that's not the truth. Actually we're feeling broken, tired, weighed down but we don't share this with our friends because we don't want to appear weak out of fear of rejection.

It's one of the most obvious traits in our society that is eating us from the inside out. We are all desperately seeking vulnerable relationships but don't know how to go about it. We are all suffering from neglecting our need to be weak with each other.

I have a friend who has an infectious way of communicating that inspires vulnerability. Often when we're having a meal with friends, she'll openly talk about her struggles with her boyfriend and replay us the conversation she was having last night. She's open about everything and isn't scared of appearing weak. What's interesting is that in her weakness, she actually projects herself as being strong. She is secure enough in herself to tell us about what she struggles with. She has a strong self-identity which means it doesn't matter what we think of her when she's vulnerable. This is profound. What's more, within a friendship group, vulnerability multiplies. When one person is weak, everyone else realises they can drop their act and be weak with one another as well. When the first person shows weakness, a true friend doesn't continue to present themselves as someone they're not. In fact, their falsification is amplified to be something quite ridiculous. When we choose to be weak with one another, it causes everyone to get off their high horse and stand on level ground.

The key to being vulnerable is to be honest. If the response you receive to being vulnerable is rejection, this is your clearest sign that the people you've surrounded yourself with aren't the best for you. But if your vulnerability is reciprocated, you will find you are with people who take you on an exciting journey of discovering the real depths of relationships.

Finally, authenticity is being yourself. Authentic is defined as: undisputed origin, not a copy and genuine. That'd be a great way to describe someone, "He's of his own origin." It wouldn't make much sense, but I love that! Being your own origin is being yourself. In our culture of competition, there's an increasing temptation to present ourselves as someone we're not. We hide ourselves behind a wall of insecurity as we try to convince people we are different from who we are. The key to being authentic is being fully yourself in each moment. What does that look like? It is choosing to be present and intentional rather than holding a little bit of yourself back.

> When we don't know how to deal with our weaknesses, we certainly won't know what to do with other people's weaknesses.

It's not confining to what people expect of you, but being yourself. There's an impulse to stop ourselves from being real and instead present a 'front' which is exactly the opposite of what people want to see.

Authenticity isn't hanging your feelings and emotions on a billboard for everyone to see. It's showing your true self in appropriate situations. For example, you can still be authentic in your work place but this may look different from how you are being authentic around your friends. You can be fully yourself and fully present, but you need to use discernment in how this looks. It wouldn't be appropriate to unload all of your emotional struggles whilst meeting with your line manager but this would be appropriate with your family.

Authentic people express their opinions even though they might differ from the majority. They allow their friends to show their true selves. They search for depth in conversations. They support others and sincerely wish for people to grow. They don't fake their feelings. They don't worry about pleasing everyone. They don't compare their journeys with others and they don't seek validation. Authentic people don't get jealous of other people's successes; but rather praise them. They are content being themselves. Does this paragraph describe you?

To recap, refocusing the lens through which you view life is necessary if you want to live adventurously. Refocusing is adjusting the way you view people, society and how you engage with it. What I'm trying to communicate is that there is an alternative from which you've been nurtured and influenced by culture. We've been told that ugly is wrong, community is not needed and vulnerability is a weakness.

Living adventurously is not defaulting to the rules of culture but forming a better understanding of the beauty of humans and how we live together. There is so much more we can experience if we choose to look below the surface; to chase the wonder in each other; to drop our act and find true intimacy in our friendships again. We need to be vulnerable, authentic and see people in the right way if we wish to live adventurously.

Eleven

Being Secretly Incredible

If I were to describe the characteristic of someone who lived adventurously, it would be secretly incredible. Being secretly incredible is not seeking the attention and approval of friends, but doing what you are passionate about, even when no one sees you. It's building up people around you without seeking their acknowledgement or approval.

My friend James, the same guy who gave me the bank statement so I could go to New Zealand, is secretly incredible. For as long as I've known James, he's been a friend I can trust and have fun with. James hates having a job, not because he's lazy, but because he loves people. He invests his life in befriending people suffering from homelessness and addictions. It was a privilege to share a year with James whilst we did an internship in Plymouth. I've never met a man who's as selfless and generous as James is. He's the kind of guy who will stop and talk to any stranger in the street because he doesn't believe in labelling and judging people. James doesn't often use social media, he wears simple clothes and wouldn't stand out in a crowd. He carries a deep voice and a husky infectious laugh. When I'm with him, James often asks, "Luke, how are you *really* doing?" He isn't interested with the surface level friendship but instinctively seeks a heart felt companionship. James probably wouldn't agree with being called secretly incredible, but I know anyone who has spent time with him would agree with the description.

I have felt temptations to seek recognition, appreciation and affirmation from my peers. I've dipped my toe into this culture and it feels surprisingly good. A feeling of being loved and wanted, though only superficially. Every time this lifestyle pulls me further in, there is something that shouts within me, "NO!" My inner voice tells me that this culture of seeking approval won't satisfy. A culture of looking trendy and hanging with the 'cool kids' won't fulfil me. Instead, what I want to be is secretly incredible. Let me explain why I think you should too.

Seeking approval over excellence has twisted motives. Consider those areas of your life where you wish someone knew how thoughtful or caring you were. I have felt this before. Moments where I wished my friends could see how brilliant I am because I've helped a stranger in the street. Times where I would put in the extra effort at work but received no praise for it. My parents didn't relocate to South Korea as missionaries because they wanted people to think they were amazing. They identified a need and realigned their lives to meet that need - that's secretly incredible.

I have a hunch that some of the most incredible people that have sacrificed their lives for a greater cause are people we'll never hear about. There won't be books written about their lives. Their legacy will live on because of the countless lives they'll have touched - but we'll never hear about them because they sought greatness over appreciation.

This idea of seeking praise is ingrained in us from an early age. I remember as a child, every time I wanted to impress my father by jumping off a wall, kicking a ball or cycling with no hands, I would shout, "Dad! Look at me!" Craving recognition is a defence mechanism to feel valued and appreciated. For young children it's second nature and normal to seek acceptance from parents, but as adults, it's a mechanism we're reluctant to let go of.

In a world driven by self-promotion, Jesus gave us a perfect example of something different. After he raised a young girl from the dead he told her, "Tell no one." Later he healed a man with leprosy and said again, "Tell no one." Jesus healed two blind guys and instructed them, "Say nothing to anyone." Jesus, at this time of his ministry, was not interested in recognition. Or for that matter, I can't think of a single time he sought the approval and validation from anyone. He was secure in who he was.

I mentioned my parents briefly but it's probably worth explaining a little more about why they're incredible. As far back as I can remember my parents were in debt. My father had co-owned a car parts business with a friend that went bust. I have a clear memory of helping my mother cut up credit cards on the kitchen counter. At eight years of age, I had no idea what I was doing. The debt caused my parents to reassess what they valued in life. They chose to put their kids first which meant the four of us would get new clothes and school equipment before my parents got anything.

My parents wore the same clothes year after year; my father drove a 1997 Ford Escort and my mother very rarely got a haircut. For a short while I even remember my father posting an advertisement in the local Post Office to iron clothes for people. For a few months we ironed this one man's clothes and it was my job to iron his underwear (I had to earn my pocket money somehow). My family were strapped for cash and my parents fought hard to do what they could to give their children an ordinary upbringing. Though, in hindsight, ironing someone else's underwear isn't normal for an eight year old!

My mother was a primary school teacher and my father worked at a telesales call centre. How my mother was a school teacher, ran a swimming club and raised four children, I'll never know. We all knew that my father didn't enjoy working at the call centre. As a loving husband and a caring father, he knew he would have to graft hard just to pay bills and provide food. As my sisters began to leave home and my brother signed up to the Marines, the stress on my parents ever slowly decreased and they were able to pay off their debt. They updated our outdated home and it was a historic day when they finally ripped out the 80's style kitchen to install a modern one.

One summer they sent my brother to a summer youth camp and the following year my father volunteered in the camp kitchen. The youth camp had guest speakers in the evening and on a Wednesday evening there was a mission speaker who talked about the different mission opportunities and needs around the world. The seed was planted in my father who had been sat in the tent with the other volunteers. The following year my mother joined to help with the admin and also heard the mission speakers share about their adventures and the need for people to go overseas. The following year my parents had their house up for sale.

It took two more years to sell the house, meanwhile they quit their jobs and signed up with the mission organisation WEC (World Evangelism for Christ). Because they did not have any mission experience they were sent to a mission school in Canada where they spent six months studying. After studying at a Bible college and training for cross-cultural living, their placement was in South Korea where they taught English in a Korean mission school (a lot of Koreans are required to speak English before they can go oversees).

My parents returned to the WEC headquarters in London and considered their options. Now they had quit their full-time jobs, sold their home and were now living on financial support, there was little for them to do in England.

A secretly incredible lifestyle is doing what you do for those who matter most to you and for the needs of those around you.

They returned back to South Korea and continued working in different Christian schools that needed English teachers. My parents lived in South Korea for 10 years and still consider it their home. They would be foolish to think the missionary lifestyle would be a fast track way to be recognised. Instead they are humbly served South Koreans to improve their English. My parents, Kim and Paul, live adventurous lives because they don't seek affirmation, appreciation, or accreditation; instead they seek to live secretly incredible lives.

Bob Goff hits the nail on the head in *Love Does* when he writes, "I don't think Jesus wants us to make a fashion statement or be edgy by promoting ourselves on the backs of clothing and bracelets all the time either. I think instead, Jesus wants us to write "Be Awesome" on an undershirt where it won't be seen, not on the back of a hoodie." That's what adventurous living looks like.

Being secretly incredible isn't trying to promote yourself. This would be contradictory. A secretly incredible lifestyle is doing what you do for those who matter most to you and for the needs of those around you. It's not only about building an organisation, developing a creative mission statement, wearing political t-shirts or moaning to every other person about what you think is wrong with the world. A secretly incredible person just gets on with it. That's the key. It's just getting on with life; prudently considering how you can have an impact on those around you and on a local and global scale… and just doing it.

My friend Joe is a guy who gets this. Joe lives in Bali, Indonesia where he leads a training school (called YWAM: Youth With A Mission) for those who want to do mission work. As well as leading, teaching and training, Joe started his own ministry called Traffic Light Ministry. The more time Joe spent in Bali, where he learnt the local language and adapted to the culture, he began to witness the desperate poverty and mass neglect of children on the street. A lot of the children are forced by their parents or owners to beg on the street corners. In the evening they would locate themselves near the traffic lights and street lamps as this would be the only way they'd been seen by people passing by.

Joe, the passionate and authentic guy he is, decided to do something about this and began meeting with the children each week. With no hidden agenda he'd spend his evenings with unwanted and unloved children. He'd play sports with them, teach them to sing songs and they would teach him to dance the Balinese way.

Joe doesn't post filtered photos on Instagram or boast about how many children he met each week. He doesn't seek the approval of his friends at home, nor does he seek a title or position. Instead, he gets his hands and feet dirty as he sits on the road side with unwanted children. This is being secretly incredible. It's not how we present ourselves but the condition of our heart. It's about what goes on inside of us and our motivation to love those around us. Joe isn't interested in how many likes he gets on Facebook, he's interested in changing lives.

What I love about James, my parents and Joe is that they don't seek status, importance or acknowledgment. They aren't interested in money, fame or lots of followers. They're mature enough to realise the rat race is not worth the hassle. Their experiences have taught them there is an alternative to seeking the ordinary life. It is possible to be happy and live with purpose. They understand Jesus' model of not telling everyone what they are doing. Their lives define adventure.

This is what the secretly incredible life looks life. It's about being awesome. It's being yourself and doing what you're good at. Seeking excellence in the mundane. Committing your life for the sake of others. Not talking about everything you've done.

Our life doesn't need to be like a promo video that constantly shows the highlight reel. That would be boring. As I've mentioned, what we all crave is authenticity from each other. Authenticity is sharing the real everyday life with each other. The highs and the lows. Perhaps more than a big travelling trip, a new enterprise, a new product or a bucket list with exciting dreams - adventurous living is choosing to live genuine and raw lives with those around you.

"There's trouble ahead when you live only for the approval of others, saying what flatters them, doing what indulges them. Popularity contests are not truth contests—look how many scoundrel preachers were approved by your ancestors! Your task is to be true, not popular." - Jesus (Luke 6:26 MSG)

Twelve

Doing Life Together

To bring these thoughts to a close, it's worth summarising the journey so far. I believe if we are able to relinquish our comforts for a lifestyle of adventure we will find a deeper meaning and purpose. When we take a few risks, small or big ones, we will experience the vibrancy and excitement that life offers. It's likely we have stayed in our comfort zones for so long that we don't know what taking risks feels like anymore. When we take risks it will certainly add more colour to our lives.

What is lacking in many of us is the self-belief that we can actually achieve our goals and dreams. It's understandable as life throws whatever it can to discourage and distract us.

Hold true to your values and what is true about yourself. Remind yourself what you are good at and keep pushing yourself to achieve more.

Fear is the biggest barrier to overcome to live adventurously. The fear of the unknown, the fear of failure, the fear of losing, looking silly, making mistakes… the list is endless. One of the keys to overcoming fear is having courage. Courage is facing your giants, courage is befriending your doubts and worries, courage is walking into challenges that come your way. The fullness of life can't be experienced by living fearfully but only when you are courageous enough to go out and find it.

When we pursue adventures, there will be many decisions to make. This will test our willingness, desire and discernment. Saying yes will lead you down paths you never knew existed. One of those decisions may be about family. It's important to understand how our family influences the decisions we make and whether we allow them to become a barrier or a spring board to discovering more of life. Along the way it's likely you'll face opposition in all forms, in many different ways and for reasons you can't predict. People will try to stop you from achieving what you want. This gives you more of a reason to stand firm. Use these occasions to reassess and reevaluate what you believe in and build on those values.

Don't allow these negative experiences to distort your view of humanity. Instead, refocus the way you view the people around you. Look to encourage and build up friends, seek ways to serve, find the best in people and promote this in them. There's beauty in people, even if we don't see it straight away. During this process, learn to say no. Saying yes will lead you into new experiences, but without any limits or boundaries you will find yourself adventure-fatigued. Say no when it doesn't align with your values or passions. Say yes when it does.

Last but not least, just be incredible. Be you. Be authentic and vulnerable with the people around you. There's no need to gloat or boast and social media won't fulfil your desire for connection. Be proud of what you have achieved and share that with those who care. Finally, there's one more aspect of adventurous living and that's doing life together.

Adventures are best when they are experienced and shared with close friends. Memories are often the building blocks for a friendship; sharing the highs and lows of life with those around you who care makes it all worthwhile.

When I studied in New Zealand for a year and later in the Netherlands for a second year, I felt very much alone. Whilst I spent my time with the other students, I didn't invest into the friendships like I should have because I knew it would be unlikely I would ever see them again. I was resistant to share and build memories. These two years taught me the importance of valuing close friends and making the most of each moment, regardless of how long you'll spend together. I believe that life is more fun when it's shared with those you love.

An event called Tough Mudder illustrates this point well. It is a twelve-mile mud-run made up of 21 obstacles that is designed to test your physical and mental abilities while pushing you to the edge of your comfort zone.

Will Dean created Tough Mudder as a business to help people rediscover fun. Writing in *It Takes A Tribe*, he identifies that we spend more time behind computers and communicating through devices rather than being outside and speaking with one another. Tough Mudder is counter-cultural in the sense that it gets you covered in mud and speaking to strangers you've never met. It pushes you past the boundaries of not caring what you look like and helping people who look even worse than you.

> Adventures are best when they are experienced and shared with close friends.

Will goes on to suggest that a Tough Mudder event represents something of life, where we can work as hard as we want but can still never predict what's ahead. "The thing about life, and about business, is that however hard you prepare for it, however ready you make yourself, there will be plenty waiting around the corner to de-rail you. Tough Mudder as an event dramatises that fact: it is about expecting the unexpected and about owning your fears."

One of the stories shared in this book that particularly impacted me was about Randy Pierce. You can also find a video shared on YouTube which captures the moment Randy stood on a platform preparing for an obstacle called King of the Swingers. On the obstacle you have to jump out to grab a trapeze bar, eight feet away from the platform. When you have reached the full arch of the swing you then reach out to hit a bell, before plunging into the cold water below.

It's worth mentioning that Randy lost most of his sight when he was 22 years old to a rare neurological disease and later became totally blind. The same disease affected his spine and he was wheelchair-bound. Not deterred by his physical limitations, Randy has since completed four marathons and climbed the forty-eight mountains in New Hampshire. In the video you can see Randy measuring the distance with his walking stick and trying to make the calculations to know when to let go. He leaped from the platform, fuelled with adrenaline, and over shot the trapeze but still clung on and somehow hit the bell before falling into the water. It's an incredible story of overcoming the fears and barriers that prevent us from living adventurously.

Moreover, Randy is surrounded by a team of friends that help him get around the course. More often than not, Randy uses his size and strength to help his team mates get over obstacles they wouldn't be able to themselves. There's no reason to allow a physical limitation stop us from helping each other, nor should we refuse help from someone who is different from ourselves.

Having done two Tough Mudder mud-runs myself, there is an element of truth that the obstacles you have to overcome represent the curve balls that life throws at us. There were times during the courses when I felt like I didn't have much left and there were some obstacles where it would have been impossible to climb over by myself. I needed my team mates to help me overcome them, whilst I was also there for them. That's how a Tough Mudder works, you require help from the people around you.

This is the same with life. We need one another. It reminds me of the story of the Brownlee brothers who were competing in the 2016 World Series triathlon in Mexico that consisted of a gruelling 1500m swim, followed by 40km cycle and a 10km run. Jonny Brownlee was winning the race with only 700 metres left, until complete exhaustion took over him and his legs began to wobble. He was looking behind him to see where the other competitors were, whilst swerving from side to side, struggling to hold himself up. Alistair, his brother was running in third place closely behind a South African competitor. Alistair instinctively grabbed his brother and continued running, propping him up. Arm in arm, the Brownlees crossed the finished line in second and third as Jonny collapsed on the floor to receive medical attention. In an interview afterwards, a reporter asked Alistair, "There's some people speculating whether that's actually legal, I don't think you cared did you? It seemed like a natural human reaction to your brother." Alistair replied humbly, "Yeah, obviously a natural human reaction to my brother, but to be honest, anyone in that position I would have done the same thing."

That's what doing life together looks like. Alistair Brownlee could have seen that his brother was struggling as an opportunity to overtake him and possibly win the race.

Instead, he compromised his race time and position to help his brother in need. Doing life together is holding loosely to our own ambitions and goals and focusing our attention on the needs of those around us.

We all have gifts and skills to offer that others would benefit from. It's dangerous to run on ahead without looking back to offer a hand to those who are behind you. Moreover, it's prideful to not to grab the hand that is reaching out offering help. Even when we are (metaphorically) covered in mud, we can't afford to judge one another because we're all in this together. Adventurous living is selfless living. Putting your own needs second to those around you.

In the Bible there was a guy called Paul who was in prison but still wrote letters to his friends, he instructed them, "Do nothing from selfish ambition or conceit, but in humility count others more significant that yourselves. Let each of you look not only to his own interests, but also to the interests of others." (Philippians 2:3-4) That is how a community functions, how a family lives and a relationship works. Doing life together is living adventurously.

Top Tips

Here's some practical, though not exhaustive, ideas to help you live adventurously.

Serve. Find a group you are passionate about and offer to help out. Even if it's serving tea or distributing food. You'll find more meaning to life when you do something you find purpose in.

Read. Try and read a challenging or inspiring book once month. Teach yourself something new. Motivate yourself by someone else's story.

Encourage. Be intentional about encouraging others around you. Invest your life in others and they will do the same.

Be authentic. People want to know you for who you are. Be yourself. Celebrate your differences and accept yourself as you are.

Say yes. Say yes to the small decisions and you'll slowly find it easier to make those life-changes choices.

Travel. When possible, go and see more of the world. Use contacts you have around the world to save money and see the local culture. There are also many agencies and organisations that allow you to travel and serve communities short or long term.

Learn. Keep teaching yourself new things. Start an evening course. Retrain in something you're passionate about. Go to a new group. Buy books on a topic.

Connect. Reduce your screen time and connect with people in real conversation. Arrange to meet a friend for a coffee regularly.

Challenge yourself. Set yourself goals each month or each year. Sign up for a half-marathon or a Tough Mudder. Start a new hobby. Reconnect with old friends. Give yourself something to look forward to and to work towards.

Think bigger. In your work, think bigger than your 9 to 5. Are there charities that could use your skills? Could you travel and work? Could you start your own business? Dream bigger than what you already know. Research and ask around.

Go outdoors. Even if you're a city lover, spend more time in the countryside. Reconnect with the quietness and solitude. Embrace the stillness and beauty.

Give. Give your time to someone on the street who looks lost. Give your money to a cause you care about. Give your resources to a friend who needs them. Give your ideas to a work colleague.

Don't be busy. Remember your boundaries so you can focus on the most important things. Avoid just filling your time so you are too busy. You'll miss out on a lot. Even if your life is full, try not to be busy.

Discover. Find new hobbies. Find new books. Find new friends. Find a new coffee shop, a new country walk, a new recipe. Keep discovering new things.

Research. Search for the best things to do in a city you've not been to. Use TripAdvisor to choose the best park, the best coffee shop and the best restaurant. Then you'll have a day trip planned.

Love. Finally, love those around you. Spent times with loved ones. Set aside time to do this or you'll overlook it. Loved ones are those that will stick by you through the thick and thin.

Thirteen

Epilogue

I'll let you into a little secret. I started writing this book in 2015 when I was going through an introspective time in life. I was reflecting a lot and began writing my thoughts down. I began categorising them into areas that were preventing me from doing life well and lessons I've learnt that helped me make the most of life. But it began to feel like there wasn't any purpose in writing. Although it was an extension of my journaling, why was I spending so much time put my thoughts onto paper?

In 2016 I met Harriet, my wife. Well obviously at the time she wasn't. But as our relationship grew and we began to discuss marriage, I returned back to my thoughts and figured

I would challenge myself to print them into a book and give it to her as part of my proposal. I felt I wanted to give her a gift that showed my intent in living healthily and to give something of a mandate to try live our lives by.

Romantic huh? We both laugh about it now, how innocent and a bit cheesy it was to give my wife a book as a proposal (and a ring! Don't worry, I didn't forget a ring.) But knowing I was going to print my thoughts into a book for her gave me a purpose and motivation to finish it. At the time I was in contact with a publisher, but they weren't interested, which is understandable. After all, JK Rowling was rejected 12 times before a publisher took on Harry Potter, so it didn't bother me too much.

Now with the birth of my daughter, our first child, it's given me another drive to revisit these thoughts again. Thinking of my daughter as the reader, I've refreshed and edited each chapter to be more succinct. I've used this opportunity to think, what advice or encouragement would I give my daughter to live adventurously? How can I share lessons I've learnt and challenge her to find her own purpose?

I also hope you've found it useful too.

If it isn't clear by now, the whole idea of adventurous living is to find purpose and meaning in every day life. Whether you're a data analyst or a social worker, you can live each day with adventure. The process of doing so is by redefining what purpose means for you. For some their purpose is their family, their children's future, building a brand or leaving a legacy. For others it's caring for the less fortunate and giving their finances or time. Whatever your purpose is, it's important that it's meaningful to you. My aim is to have identified some of the barriers you may experience, as well as ways to inspire and encourage you.

Having shared some of my own journey and given examples of others, the narrative is now handed over to you.

Perhaps you're not needing or ready for a complete life overhaul, but it's possible there's a few tweaks you could apply to making your life more meaningful. Reread the 'top tips', is there a couple that you could focus on this week? Don't bite off more than you can chew, make your goals manageable.

There's two questions that I have found invaluable in answering to finding purpose:

1. If finances and geographic location weren't an issue, what would you dream of doing with your life?

2. If you woke up tomorrow and one thing had changed about your life, what would it be?

All too often we limit ourselves because of finance and our location. But if these weren't a challenge for you, what would you love to do with your life? Begin to allow yourself to dream. If you woke up tomorrow and one thing had changed, what would you like it to be? I find this question challenging but insightful. Your first answer, the gut response, is usually the most accurate. Be honest with yourself. By navigating these two questions, you're already on the way to living with more purpose and living adventurously.

Thanks for reading,

Luke

P.S. If you found this book useful, why not give it to a friend? Or tell them to get their own copy!

> "The noblest art is that of making others happy."
>
> - PT Barnum

Printed in Great Britain
by Amazon